GONE RUSTIC

By CECIL ROBERTS

Novels

PILGRIM COTTAGE
SPEARS AGAINST US
BARGAIN BASEMENT
HAVANA BOUND
PAMELA'S SPRING SONG
INDIANA JANE
SCISSORS
SAILS OF SUNSET
THE LOVE RACK
LITTLE MRS. MANNINGTON
SAGUSTO
GOOSE FAIR

Belles-Lettres

GONE RUSTIC
COLLECTED POEMS
THE DIARY OF RUSSELL BERESFORD

Autobiography

HALF WAY

Gone Rustic

by
Cecil Roberts

Illustrations by
PERCY HOME

D. APPLETON-CENTURY COMPANY
INCORPORATED
NEW YORK   LONDON
1934

PRINTED IN THE UNITED STATES OF AMERICA

CONTENTS

CHAPTER   PAGE

I. FIRST THE SEED 11

II. THE COTTAGE IS FOUND 21

III. A TRIAL TRIP 41

IV. A SALE IS HELD 65

V. SOME TIPS FROM TILLY 81

VI. WISE BIRDS 101

VII. TULIPPOMANIA 129

VIII. A MONARCH COMES TO STAY 143

IX. MR. CHAUCER, KING CHARLES, AND THE
BLACKSMITH 161

X. BRICKLAYING 185

XI. THE QUITE NAKED TRUTH 203

XII. THE MISERABLE WORM 225

XIII. CONCERNING PLINY AND PLOT 237

XIV. OCTOGENARIA 265

XV. COTTAGE SECRETS 277

XVI. TRESPASSERS 295

XVII. DA CAPO 313

ILLUSTRATIONS

FACING PAGE

Pilgrim Cottage 28

The study 122

Our fireplace, from south room 198

Old fireplace, dining-room 288

CHAPTER I

FIRST THE SEED

It was in Florida that a sudden desire possessed me for a cottage in England. I had never before wanted anything as on that sunny Christmas Day I wanted a cottage in the English countryside. It was strange that I should be thirty-five before I became enthusiastically English and felt the desire to possess the Englishman's heritage, a view of friendly hills, green fields, and an old garden with phlox, honeysuckle, lavender and roses.

Why the desire should be so strong at this particular moment I could not say. I was enjoying everything that the heart could desire. Here was a land bright with sunshine. The town where I was a guest was a fairyland, dotted with miniature lakes. The red brick roads were bordered with live-oaks and festooned with hanging mosses. The hedgerows were vivid with the scarlet flame-vine. Each morning we cantered over the loamy scrub, emerging upon neat plantations of orange groves. They swept to the horizon in orderly rows, their metallic green leaves glinting in the sun. The fruit hung in yellow globes of light, oranges, tangerines and, at the base of these toylike trees, the large grapefruit which every Britisher is so anxious to give his American guest for breakfast, in the belief that his day opens with this acid overture.

Two days before Christmas we had bathed on Daytona Beach, sunning ourselves on that long shining strand devoted to speed records. Behind, on the Halifax River, our little yacht had taken us down to the silver inlet of the sea, where the flamingoes spread their pink-tipped wings. Evening brought a glory of gold and turquoise above the reach of sapphire water. There had been memorable experiences in that week; the white arc of Havana riding towards me across the azure sea; the illimitable light of the Florida Keys; the dawn coming up with a cry of wildfowl over Halifax River, as I waited on the rim of the world for the car that was to meet the New-York-bound sleeping-coach; but the culmination came with my afternoon excursion into the very realm of the dear good Queen, into the era of antimacassars, mutton-chop sleeves and handlebar whiskers.

We had lunched, on December the twenty-fourth, on the terrace of my host's house, sunblinds drawn against the glare, looking out on the circular lake through an arbour of roses. Would I like to visit some English neighbours who had an orange grove thirty miles distant? The family had settled there forty years ago. My host, I thought, disguised a feeling of mirth at the thought of them. "They are very worthy people," said my hostess, reproving the sons of the house, whose only contribution to the testimonial had been, "Oh boy!" I surmised then the ordeal before me, but not the pathos of it. Clearly it was a duty to visit old Mrs. Martin, the Misses Sophie and Katie Martin, and Master John Martin. They came of an old English family, were very retiring, but always overjoyed at the visit of a fellow-countryman. "You're for it," cried the irrepressible Walter. "Well, I'm shooting alligators with Hank.   Mother's got you chained."

By telephone we learned that Mrs. Martin would be very pleased to see us for afternoon tea.   I felt cheered at meeting again so dear an English institution.   I had carried a tea-pot and a tin of 'Earl Grey Mixture' to Venice, Tunis, Berlin and Copenhagen, mystifying the breed of page-boys who had been summoned for hot water, and had stood wide-eyed before the rite of in-fusion.   But here I had been deprived of my particular tea owing to the ignorance of a friend.   Commissioned in a last-hour rush before the departure of the boat-train to procure the aromatic mixture, he had returned, after a wild excursion through London's tobacco shops, with two pounds of 'Carlyle Mixture,' named after a scribe who was neither a tea-drinker nor an Earl.

On arrival at the house in the orange groves we were shown into the drawing-room.   Unlike most American drawing-rooms it had a door, an unnecessary thing in steam-heated houses.   This house of wooden construc-tion, with its covered verandahs and outer doors guarded by a wire mesh, making of the house a gigantic meat-safe, had no steam heating.   Here in the Florida wilds, the drawing-room proclaimed its nationality by a fire-place, a truly Victorian fireplace, with bow grate and side tiles covered with a design of unimaginable flowers climbing in bilious vertigo.

The room was unique.   The moment the black butler had ushered us in, I studied it, until my absorp-tion was broken by the advent of our hostess.   It possessed all that a modern biographer finds necessary for the derision of the Victorian era.   There were bamboo flower stands, on which the bland aspidistra reproved the exotic plant life of Florida. There was a large mirror over the plush-covered mantelpiece, a mirror on whose face there must have passed a thousand images of brooch-bearing bosoms, flowered bonnets, stock-ties, side-whiskers and dog-kennel watchchains. How many a gas or candle-lit chandelier had scintillated in that mercurial palimpsest? It had seen the young bride, departing tearfully, kissed by Papa, and the bright-faced Cornet doomed to fall at Balaclava; the golden rain of laburnum lighting the Kensington garden; the sashed child leaning to fog the surface and write with a finger her transitory name. These had come and gone ere the foreign Florida day had lit it with new visions.

The furniture, which must have been transported from England, was of the Prince Consort period. Disraeli would have found little that was unusual in this drawing-room except the gramophone that looked so unneighbourly by the piano, a fine specimen of fretwork with crimson silk panels and splay-footed brass pedals, worn away by countless performers waxing to the *fortissimo* of *Alice, Where Art Thou?*, waning to the *pianissimo* of *What Are the Wild Waves Saying?* through decades of interrogative sentiment.

And, true to the sneer of a Georgian biographer, there, on a whatnot that was not what it had been, with its lacquer chipped and mother-of-pearl lustreless, a glass dome covered a basket of fruit for ever ripe and never rotten.

A horsehair sofa with scroll ends and a mahogany back, a rotary piano stool with spindle leg, an arm-chair draped with a Paisley shawl, and an empty bird-cage, large, brassy, cluttered with rings, perches and seed receptacles, in every detail the contents of this room fitted their period. Four brutal oil portraits hung on the wall. Over the piano sat Queen Victoria, enthroned at the Crystal Palace, before an immense crowd in that monumental bird-cage.

I looked at my friends. None of us laughed. One could just as well laugh in the Egyptian Room at the British Museum. Here was a British Museum, in the heart of Florida, sustained through a civilisation of Ford cars, Spearmint chewing-gum, Woolworth's Stores, Christian Science, cocktails, jazz, greyhound racing, Rotarianism and the Ku Klux Klan. At that moment of dumb wonder the Curator entered.

Mrs. Martin was eighty-two years of age. Her son, accompanying her, was on the verge of sixty. Master John looked frail, if sunburnt, but his mother was erect, robust, of majestic port, as Pope would say. She had the arm of her son, not for support, but for dignity, one surmised. Her hair was silver, but her cheeks retained the pink that, with blue eyes, still bore report of beauty vanished. Not wholly vanished, let me add. Straight, with a quick light in her eyes, she was of that race of women we believe gone from our age, incapable of promising ourselves such sublime preservation.

Mrs. Martin greeted us, and apologised for not being present on our arrival. She always rested in the afternoon from two to four. Seated, she placed a neat foot on the stool and pulled the small table towards her. We were grouped around on odd chairs. Sophie and Katie would be in presently. "John!" cried the old lady, with a gesture. John rang the bell.

As we talked, the coloured butler, in time-green tails, appeared with an immense tray laden with a silver tea-service. It was of the massive kind one may still see occasionally, chased and crested, in a silversmith's in King Street, St. James's, or in a remote country vicarage. But their order has vanished with a race of domestic servants.

Behind the butler appeared Miss Sophie and Miss Katie with smiles and apologies. The latter was still called Baby by the old lady, although she was in the forties, stringy-necked and long-toothed. It required but a glance to see that, despite the hard work of the plantation, they were 'ladies.' Their roughened hands, their dried features and clumsily shod feet could not disguise the effect of years of refinement and safe-keeping. Poor Miss Sophie and Miss Katie, so neat, so dry, so ladylike, it was impossible to imagine that ever romance had swelled in their locket-bearing bosoms, that the bloom of youth and the blush of embarrass-ment had ever mantled their cheeks withered by the Florida sun. They sat now, stiff, smiling and attentive, on either side of their mother, while Master John, af-flicted with a twitching of his eyes, handed round the tea and thin bread and butter.

They talked of England. Mrs. Martin had lived in Somerset when a girl, and had married in London, where the four children were born. One, now a clergyman, lived in England and came on a visit every other year. Sophie, Katie and John did not remember England; they were too young when they sailed for Florida. They were always hoping to make a visit.

But there was mother and—without further words I felt confirmed in a first impression of proud poverty.

Later I learned they were scarcely wringing a living out of this soil. They would not employ modern methods. They were obstinate and fantastically conscientious in their dealings. My Florida host, a grower with a hundred thousand acres, told me he had tried in vain to help them. They had come here forty-six years ago, father and mother and family, in the hope of making a fortune and returning to England. Mr. Martin had died, hope had died, grimly they clung on to their estate while around them enterprising neighbours leapt to prosperity.

Tea finished, Mrs. Martin rose with a sprightliness that surprised me, seized a stick, and commanded me to follow. I must see her garden. A few steps, and I was back in old England. The transformation was staggering. The lawn, the rockery, the sundial, the pergola, the rose arbours and a little tiled summer-house, they were all perfect in their fidelity to the English type. Here, in the middle of the Florida groves, fighting the tropical heat of summer, the un-English warmth of winter, the human will had triumphed over Nature. "It is like an English garden, isn't it?" asked the old lady. Had it been like the Malay jungle I should have agreed. But my agreement and enthusiasm needed no hypocrisy.

"It must be nothing compared with yours," said old Mrs. Martin.

"I haven't a garden. You see I——"

She gave me a swift, keen look, sharp as an eagle. "You haven't a garden!" she cried scornfully.

"Then why are you an Englishman?"

Fierce, noble old lady, so faithful to England through forty-six years of exile!   I had no answer worthy of her question.   If she felt contempt she was too well bred to show it, but as we turned from treasure to treasure I began to realise, as never before, the legacy so firmly held by those who fear to lose it.   The butler in tails, the silver tea-service, the fretwork piano, all these things awakening my derision, were now touched with pathos.

Finally, the old lady took me into a musty study and showed me a relief map of Great Britain which she had imported at great trouble.   "When I know I shall never see England again, and the thought is unbearable, I come in here and run my fingers over this map, over the mountains and hills, down the valleys, through England, Scotland and Wales, and I think of the villages, and all the gardens they contain, and, you know, it gives me great comfort.   Oh, how can you live in England without a garden?" she cried.

Town bred, a wanderer over the earth, that question had never assailed me.   It must have been asked by that old lady at the moment when I was ripe for the experience.   All the way home, motoring through a swift, glowing sunset, the idea grew.   Impatience seized me when I thought of the sixty-two lectures, in sixty-two universities, colleges and clubs that stood between me and immediate realisation of my ambition.   I wanted then to hurry home to England, to find the house and garden, to be installed and catch the coming spring.

I had missed too many.   I would miss no more. Old Mrs. Martin had planted yet another seed.

HOMECOMING

Cliffs breaking through the haze,
    And a narrowing sea,
Soon will my eager gaze
    Have sight of thee—

England, the lovelier now
    For absence long;
Soon shall I see your brow,
    Hear a lark's song.

Heart, curb thy beating—there!
    Channel cliffs glow,
Eddystone, Plymouth, where
    Drake mounts the Hoe!

Red of the Devon loam,
    Green of the hills,
April!—and I am home,
    God, my heart thrills!

Far have I travelled and
    Great beauty seen,
But oh, out of England
    Is anywhere green?

Thankful and thankful again
    As never before,
One of the Englishmen
    Comes to his shore!

CHAPTER II

THE COTTAGE IS FOUND

I

It is easy to say, "I want a cottage in the country." There is a time in the life of every city dweller when he says this. An immediate granting of this wish would fill his mind with perplexity. What kind of cottage, in what part of the country? For most, a country habitation means a cottage. The word requires defining. Generally it is defined as 'Elizabethan,' to the disregard of personal comfort.

I shall bring on myself shouts of derision when I say civilisation reached the period of Queen Anne before we learned how to build houses that could be lived in with comfort. For exterior beauty the Tudor and the Elizabethan are cherished, but these houses have serious defects as residences. The week-end guest is seldom aware of them. He finds it jolly to crack his head on the lintels, and his visit is too short to experience the depression caused by low roofs. He does not know how high-built windows, touching the ceiling, black out the person sitting with his back to the light, or that those delightful, wide fireplaces have a fearful draught and a genius for smoking. He does not know that the fear of fire is ever present, and that the whole layout of the plan presents a hundred difficulties in domestic and social convenience. People who live in old houses never throw complaints, but they are, nevertheless, acutely aware of the drawbacks.

There is the matter of size, too. The word 'cottage' can mean anything. I have accepted a week-end invitation to stay in a small cottage, and found myself installed in a suite of rooms, with steam heating, hot and cold water, and a private bath-room. The simple-looking barn had suffered a parquet change into a ball-room, and the cowshed, Lutyenised, housed a Rolls-Royce and a lighting plant. The simple life included a telephone in every room, a cocktail before every meal, and a group of guests who played Bridge beyond midnight. One crimson-nailed lady complained bitterly that the birds made a frightful noise in the morning. But she appeared in *The Tatler* fondling a goat.

The word 'country' bears various definitions. I like my fellow men, and to lose contact with them makes me miserable. Obviously I didn't want a cottage in the heart of Wales or the Lake District, and, while I had no wish to live in a swamp, I was not prepared to live on the crest of a hill, where no window could be opened without the curtains becoming horizontal or suffering a bombardment of slamming doors. A friend of mine built a beautiful house with a beautiful view. He was blown out of it in nine months.

My idea of a country cottage was something like this:

(1) Within comfortable motoring distance of London, so that friends should have no excuse for deserting me, and when the country palled I could easily return to London.

(2) An old house, but not so old that there would be a continuous bill for repairs.

(3) A house with four bedrooms and two or three reception rooms. It must face south-west, with an eastern morning aspect.

(4) An old garden, large enough to keep a gardener employed, but not so large that I could not dispense with him if he became obstreperous, or expenses had to be cut.

(5) A house I could buy freehold, support without too severe a drain on income and retain as an addition to a place in town.

(6) Interesting country, hilly, unspoilt, with a variety of walks and stretches of woodland.

(7) A market town, picturesque if possible, within easy reach, for domestic and domestics' convenience.

(8) In or near a village not too squire, parson or county-ridden, since my presence might perturb them, and my wayward nature occasion offence.

(9) A place it gave me a joy to look at, a pride to own, and my friends a pleasure to visit.

And is that all? you may ask.

Well, I had no hope of having these conditions fulfilled. In my heart I was a little afraid of this sudden passion for a cottage in the country. I scarcely knew the name of a bird or a flower. It had been my ambition, which I had satisfied, to live in some of the great cities of the world. It was in vain that there ran in my veins the blood of ten generations of Leicestershire squires, High Sheriffs five of them, sturdy farmers, breeders of cattle and hard riders all of them.

Or was it in vain, was it the avatar working in me, the deep old passion for the land agitating me as water agitates the twig in the dowser's hands?

Whatever it was, I wrote optimistically to the estate agents of the near counties informing them that I was looking for a desirable property. I learned speedily what an amazing word 'desirable' is in a land agent's vocabulary. The postman must have thought I was running a mail-order business.

The spring, the summer, passed. My car's speedometer registered nine thousand miles. Winter found me, in the month of January, at Cannes still opening fat envelopes with lists of desirable properties. I no longer read those lists, but nothing I could do would stop them coming to me.

II

My friend S. found a wife through a puncture. He went to a house to ring up the nearest garage and the young woman who conducted him to the telephone changed her name for his within a year. I found my cottage similarly.

The next June, when all hope of that ideal cottage had vanished, I was motoring with a friend to Oxford when we suffered a puncture. I never thought it possible for anyone to enjoy a puncture so much. Removing his coat and rolling up his sleeves, my friend delved into his tool kit, and when I proffered help, firmly ordered me away with the contempt that all practical men feel for the tribe of artists. Clearly I was in the way, but pride would not permit me to be a passive spectator. I wandered off, knowing he was happy in his dirty, underhand way.

We had just left Henley-on-Thames and were mounting a considerable hill when our mishap occurred. Oxford was some twenty miles distant. At the roadside where we had stopped there was a stile and a footpath crossing a concave field. At the far side there was another stile in the hedge, and nothing but the sky beyond. That meant a view.

I climbed the stile, crossed the field, and at the second stile found I had struck a country lane. Around me the view was imposing, almost Tyrolean, with steep larch-covered hillsides, and in the distance, between thick beechwoods nobly clothing the greensward, a ravine. Somewhere below lay the road along which we had come from Henley. Instinctively I felt this was my kind of countryside, lush, hilly, slightly romantic, with hidden reserves of beauty.

Immediately below me, in the lane which twisted sharply out of sight, I saw a few chimney-pots. Instantly my curiosity was stirred. I suffer from round-the-corneritis.

> *We are the Pilgrims, master; we shall go*
> *Always a little further; it may be*
> *Beyond that last blue mountain barred with snow,*
> *Across that angry or that glimmering sea.*

There Flecker speaks for me.

How long would that puncture take? Anyhow, we had an hour in which to reach Oxford for our lunch engagement. I went over the stile and down the lane to the enticing corner. I might find there a garden or a rubbish heap.

The corner turned, I found neither. I was entering the village, if some eight houses merit that name. They were neither thatched nor of the kind that causes sub-editors to reverse the adjective and write 'Britain Beautiful' as a caption to a rustic illustration. But as cottages they would arouse enthusiasm in city-dwellers or touring Americans. Their gardens had neat privet hedges, hollyhocks, roses and clematis-covered porches. There was a communal well of beauty and utility. But something beyond, at the foot of the hill, caught my eye. A bow window jutted out on to the road, with square panes, and a sloping roof and weathered tiles. I hurried on and delight grew. The house stood slightly back from a side road. There was a large gravel clearing sufficient for a coach to turn in, a round lawn, gay with flowers, and on it a white gibbet from which dangled, no body, but a golden ball. So this was *The Golden Ball*.

Once upon a time it must have been a rest for the stage-coach. Seeing a dark, open doorway I peered in. A fat dog wagged its tail. The parlour, a low room with scrubbed floor and window seat in the bow, was empty. On the wall hung a dart-board, on the table lay a shove-ha'penny board. I could not linger, but as I left I surmised that a cheery-looking man digging in the vegetable garden across the road was mine host.

I followed the lane as it curved in a half-circle, then halted. It was time to return, but as I turned I caught a glimpse over a high hedge of a russet-tiled roof with

three black-and-white dormer windows. That was all
I could see; they just tipped the encircling hedge, a
superb testimonial to the hand of a trimmer. Then
I noticed a small green door under a clematis-burdened
porch. There was a name on it, in small faded letters.

PILGRIM COTTAGE

I stood looking at it for a few minutes, contemplating
that entrancing name. Bunyan's *Pilgrim's Progress*, the
Mayflower with its Pilgrim Fathers, the Pilgrim's Way,
the name evoked thoughts of all these.

I approached the door and was just able to peer over.
One glance, and I drew back, checking the cry on my
lips. Years ago I had been taken to see the home of
Hans Andersen in Odense. I had a preconceived no-
tion of how the house of that writer of fairy tales should
look. I found it to be a dark, mean little hovel in
a dull street.

Now, when I looked over the garden door, I knew
where he should have lived. There was a path to the
house, with a wide border on each side of London
pride, gypsophila, snapdragon, hollyhocks and lavender.
At the end of the path a rustic porch, covered with
brier rose and clematis, guarded the dark door. The
house was low and roofed with russet tiles. An absurd chimney-pot rose on a white stack at one end,
at the other the house was hidden behind an immense
yew. The front had three windows, triple paned, below, and three dormer windows, quartered, above.
The whole front was smothered beneath white brier
roses.

From the borders of the path a green lawn ran out of

view on either side, with a gnarled apple tree to the left
and a fantastically clipped yew to the right. I almost
dislocated my neck in the effort to see more. I felt
certain that only part of the fairy tale had been seen.
I must go in. Whoever lived in that house must be
pleasant to meet.

I put my hand on the latch and raised it, but the
garden door did not open. Then I saw it was fastened
with a chain and a padlock. Since the padlock was on
the outside it was obvious that the owner was away.

Baffled, I gazed longingly over the top of the door.
Why was it that other people always found these
delectable spots, and that other people never seemed
quite to deserve them? At last I dragged myself away,
and followed the line of the hedge to see if I could
get a view from another angle. To my surprise the
cottage was settled on a small island, with a lane almost
round it. A second chimney-stack appeared in view,
over an even more enchanting and crazy roof that bil-
lowed like a wave. Beyond the roof four slender
poplars decorated the sky. The cottage had a wing
at right angles.

I retraced my steps. It was maddening to be so
near yet so far from a complete survey. I quite forgot that this place had nothing to do with me, that
it was the property of someone whose name I did not
know. As I regained the lane I noticed a small gap
at the bottom of the hedge. A dog could have gone
through it. I went down on my knees to get a view of
the garden, but was frustrated by a thick bed of phlox.
I thrust my head in farther until the thorns caught my
jacket. It wasn't a minute's work to enlarge that gap

Pilgrim Cottage

and find myself, scratched but elated, through that hedge. I scrambled to my feet, a shameless trespasser.

The scene before me surpassed all expectation. A perfect green lawn ran round the house. At the back the roof descended in an unbroken sweep down to the ground. An old apple tree trailed its branches over the mellowed tiles. I could now follow the unique design of this domain. There was a round hedge, a round garden bordering it, a round lawn, and in the centre the cottage with its dormer windows and billowing roof. The wing of the house faced east, and this right-angled corner, free from the overgrowing brier, had lovely black timbering. At the foot of the main chimney-stack there was a curious brick protuberance some four feet high, overgrown with creepers, and planted on its surface with dwarf cypresses. The east side of the house, with a single window below and a dormer above, was covered with a fan-shaped vine. The garden that faced this side had a high rustic trellis smothered with crimson rambler, American pillar, and Dorothy Perkins in profuse bloom.

Seldom had I walked on such lush turf. In silence I walked round the house, and as I gained the front, there came into view the last thing needed for a complete picture of rustic felicity. Under the apple tree on the lawn was an old well, with bucket and windlass.

I paused before the dark door, with its brass Adam-design knocker. All the windows were shut fast. Should I wake the Sleeping Beauty within? And then the fairy-tale nature of this place became more real.

There was no one here, there had been no one here for a considerable time. The door had Time's seal upon it, a network of unbroken cobwebs.

If I had been more observant I should have known this from the first. It accounted for the confidence and number of the birds I had seen walking on the grass when I peered over the garden door. They were accustomed to being unmolested. This garden grew in silence.

Again I walked round the house. I looked in through the windows, shading my eyes against the light. It was difficult to see much. The interior was furnished. After a time I made out some oak beams. There was a dining-room with a large open fireplace, and a small sitting-room opening into a drawing-room, also with a wide Elizabethan fireplace. From what I could see and surmise the interior was as exciting as the exterior.

I made a final survey, counting the apple trees, ten, the yew trees, two, the poplars, four. There were also laburnum and syringa trees, and in one shady corner a splendid chestnut. The hedge was a mixture of hawthorn and variegated privet, beautifully clipped and blossoming at intervals with hawthorn, and wild rose, now in pink and white flower. The flower-beds were all edged with a deep collar of emerald thrift with purple button flowers. Some poppies flamed in a corner, there were two beds of pinks under the windows. Clumps of lupins, white, mauve and purple, competed with blue anchusa, foxgloves, giant daisies, antirrhinums, begonias and geraniums.

The garden contradicted the story of the house. Its

luxuriance and tidiness spoke of incessant care. Ignorant as I then was of the work a garden demands,
however simple, I knew that behind all this profusion
someone with untiring zeal and skilled hands had
worked, was working even now. The trimmed hedge,
the clipped yew, the smooth lawn had been disciplined
through Time.

Glancing at my wrist-watch, I started. I had become oblivious of everything except my discovery.
Whatever would my friend think? Hastily I struggled
on hands and knees through the gap in the hedge,
dusted myself and hurried away. But I called first
at *The Golden Ball*, hailing the landlord in his garden.
What he told me made my heart jump. No one was
living now at Pilgrim Cottage. The late owner was
dead. He believed it was to let, furnished. He gave
me the name of the probable agents in Henley. I
thanked him and hurried up the lane towards the stile.
It was nearly half-past twelve. We were due in Oxford at one o'clock.

As I feared, I was greeted with strong protest. The
wheel had been changed half an hour ago. He had
been looking all over the place.

"You've been gone three-quarters of an hour! What
on earth have you been doing?"

Something in my manner made him regard me suspiciously.

"Richard, I've found it!" I exclaimed.

"Found what?"

"The cottage! It's just over there. You never saw
such a place. Elizabethan, black and white, oak-
timbered, with apple trees, a lawn, a well—everything!"

"Damp, rats, rotten beams and no sanitation—yes, I know," he retorted, churlishly. "Get in!"

But I did not get in. Foreseeing opposition, I bargained.

"Listen, Richard," I said, "I can't risk losing this. The agent's in Henley. It's only ten minutes away. I want to go now."

"Then you'll walk," replied Richard, getting in. "Don't be an idiot. We're late now. We'll do it coming back. Get in!"

"No!" I said, obstinately. "I won't risk losing that place for a minute. I'm sorry, Richard, but I'm determined to see the agents now."

"But we haven't time to see the place!"

"No, but if I get the keys, no one else can."

He looked at me as though he had a petulant child to deal with.

"All right, get in," he said. "But you can make the apology for being late. I see you've a bee in your bonnet."

He turned the car. Half-way back, down the long elm-lined avenue into Henley, he broke an angry silence.

"Let me tell you something, my boy. That cottage's been to let for over a year. Two owners have died in it in two years. There's something wrong with it!"

"How do you know?" I exclaimed, surprised.

"While hunting for you, I found a pub, and had one. Thinking of you I was good enough to enquire if there were any cottages around here, and the landlord said there was one, tumbling to pieces, Olde Worlde and all that. It sounds like yours."

"Wait till you see it," I said, laconically.

We arrived at the agents'. A terrifyingly enterprising young man, with an Old Harrovian tie and an engaging smile, wanted to show me over the cottage. I explained that we were due for a luncheon engagement in Oxford. Would he let us have the keys for inspection on our way back?

He agreed reluctantly. "Don't crack your head on the beams," he said, warningly, as we left.

III

When we unlocked the door the musty smell of all long-closed houses assailed us. We stepped straight into the dining-room. It was furnished with a hideous Tudoresque buffet, a gate-legged table and some rush-bottomed chairs. Over the immense open fireplace there was a gun rack with a powder cupboard in the corner. The ceiling was supported by one heavy oak beam that crossed it with a fantastic warp. An old door led into a dark pantry. A narrow staircase wound up out of sight. Another door brought us into a tiny sitting-room with a window looking on to the garden front. The ceiling was oak-beamed, like an agent's advertisement. We pressed on into the drawing-room, low, oblong, with a wide window looking on to the trellis of rambling roses. This ceiling was also oak-beamed. There was a wide Elizabethan fireplace. A small side-window overlooked a bed of lilies and the lawn at the back.

"Wouldn't this give an American joy!" exclaimed Richard. "Hello, look at this!"

In the wall at the back of the fireplace there was an iron door. He opened it, revealing a deep bake-oven. The abutment I had seen in the garden, with the dwarf cypresses growing on it, was explained.

"It looks to me as if this had once been two cottages. This small sitting-room was the scullery. The copper was there," said Richard, pointing to a concave space in the wall where a vase stood. "No cottage would have two fireplaces this size."

"I've been told that the most important part is the kitchen—let's look at it," I said, retracing my steps through the dining-room. Another door led into the kitchen. It had a pleasant view of the garden. A door took us down five steps into a cool dairy. It was under the roof I had seen sloping down to the lawn.

"Just what I thought," exclaimed Richard, returning.

"Delightful, isn't it?" I agreed.

He gave me a withering look.

"My dear fellow, haven't you realised the most important thing of all's missing—there's no lavatory!"

This was certainly a blow.

"But there must be!" I insisted, recovering. "You couldn't——"

"You agree this cottage is Elizabethan?"

"Why, yes."

"Then do you think Sir John Harington lived here?"

"Sir John Harington—who was he?" I demanded in bewilderment.

"He was one of the greatest benefactors who ever

lived. He flirted with Queen Elizabeth, and trans-
lated the indecent parts of *Orlando Furioso,* to her
annoyance. But most important of all, he invented
the water-closet. I don't think he came here. You'll
find what you find on every City man's notepaper—
E.C."

Well did I know those ominous letters. How many
enticing descriptions from agents had ended, almost
casually. "Sanitation—E.C."

But I was in no mood to be dashed by an earth-
closet.

"I can build a bath-room and lavatory," I said.

"And spoil the design of the house," retorted Richard.
"Let's go upstairs."

I led the way eagerly. The stairs were narrow, but
we emerged on to a landing of surprising length. I
opened a door on the right and gave an exclamation of
triumph. There were a lavatory, a basin with hot and
cold water-taps and a bath-room! Richard was over-
whelmed.

We explored farther. There was a narrow bedroom
on the left, with a dormer window built out on the
long sloping roof, a little room at the end of the landing,
also with a dormer window, and some fine beams in the
wall, and then, in a turn that took us round the upper
part of the great chimney-stack, the largest room of all,
with two windows. But what a room! The ceiling
over the window was bent like a bow. Three hundred
years of warping under the suns of England had not
left a level square yard of ceiling. A lattice window
gave an enchanting view of a steep, rising larchwood.
Another view from the dormer window looked on a

great beechwood sweeping to the sky. The house rode like a galleon in the trough of green waves. From the landing we saw a frieze of Jersey cows browsing on the steep hillside.

A cry came from Richard, who had gone back into the bedroom.

"Come here—look at that," he said.

There was a radiator by the wall! We laughed together at this incongruous object in a peasant's cottage.

"Will you take a pound bet?" asked Richard.

"What on?"

"That whoever lived here wasn't English!"

"Don't be silly——"

"Will you?" demanded Richard.

"Yes."

"Whoever lived here was an American. Only an American would think of a bath-room and steam heating in a place like this!"

I began to think he was right. Downstairs I knew he was. On the wall some verses, hand engraved, were framed.

> *In a lovely English hamlet*
> *Some three hundred years ago,*
> *Elizabethan craftsmen wrought*
> *As they so well know how,*
> *With oak and adze, with brick and lime,*
> *And flints mixed in like a crazy quilt,*
> *Nigh Pick Purse Lane and Asser's Don,*
> *'Twixt Henley Town and Stonor Park*
> *A cosy chimney cot they built.*

About that time from an English port
A Pilgrim ventured daringly
To seek religious freedom
In the New World oversea.
Now a homeward-flown descendant
Of that self-same Pilgrim dwells,
'Midst flowers and birds and sheltering hills,
In peace and sweet security,
Within those mellowed walls.

Bad enough for a very modern poet, I felt, but home-made, doubtless, with affectionate ownership shining through.

"I owe you a pound," I said to Richard.

"Spend it on seeds," he replied, derisively. "Seriously, you're not going to take this place?"

"If I can I shall buy it. It's what I've been looking for."

"I agree it's attractive—but when did you get this country cottage mania?"

"A year last Christmas, in Florida," I answered. "I was taken to tea with an old English settler. She was eighty-two, and all she could talk about was England and its gardens. When I said I hadn't got one she could hardly hide her disgust. 'You haven't a garden! Then why are you an Englishman?' she cried. I've wanted one badly ever since."

"But you've wanted a palazzo in Venice, an *appartement* in Paris, a nest in New York and a flat in London. I never knew such a fellow!" cried Richard.

"I've not always had what I wanted, but I'm going to have this," I retorted obstinately.

"Then for goodness' sake rent it first. You'll have had enough at the end of a wet summer. And I'd like the large bedroom when I come to stay."

I made no answer. I wanted to get back to the agents'.

THE OLD COTTAGE

"Is there anyone at home?" I cried,
  Lifting the knocker high,
But when the last echo died
  Not a soul made reply.

Out of the porch overhead
  Flew a startled bird;
I knocked, as to waken the dead,
  Not a footfall stirred.

In the silence I heard the call
  Of a hidden thrush,
The old house slept, over all
  A deep noonday hush.

Was I the ghost at the door,
  A century late
Since quick feet crossed the floor,
  Life passed at the gate?

"Leave me to crumble," it seemed
  The old cottage said,
"I am all that a lover dreamed,
  And my lover's dead!"

CHAPTER III

A TRIAL TRIP

I

WITHIN two weeks' time I was living in Pilgrim Cottage. When I was in America a fierce controversy was raging, owing to a professor having advocated 'companionate marriages.' The very young were all in favour, but really shrewd young women were not; they knew the fickle male who only wanted a lease, and they insisted on a freehold as the price of virginity. Cautious, I took my cottage on a three months' lease, with an option later of the freehold. This was to be a trial trip. I possessed my fair bride of quietness in July, just as the roses were fading from the house and the lavender was coming into scent.

The house was furnished. No human being was ever content with another's furniture. Like birds we are only happy in our own nests. There were several pieces of furniture that worked me up to a great loathing. There was a box-spring bed that would not spring, but was prepared to box. It threw me out on to the floor on three successive nights. I found later that the floor fell five inches towards the window. Four bricks restored the bed level, but I woke each morning at six o'clock, blamed the birds, the coffee the night before, the country air, and a farmer's cows, and then found that the bed was so placed that the first ray of the morning sun struck one's face at an angle through the curtain. The bed, therefore, was moved, and required five, four, two and one brick at each corner to maintain the level.

A house which has not been lived in for a year has a variety of smells. It also has a multitude of spiders. At night when the lamps were lit they marched across the floor, walls and ceilings in legions. Generations of them were entrenched in the curtains, in the rafters and behind the bookcases. Finally, I had all the furniture and furnishings put out on the lawn and led a grand charge of charwomen.

All this was in the nature of fun. If any hotel had dared to house me in such conditions I should have left, publishing my indignation. I endured and enjoyed all this in the same manner that people with comfortable houses find it delightful to experience the discomfort of picnics.

Being a temporary resident I procured a temporary servant. I was informed there were a number of 'ladies' who would 'oblige.' I could have endured their being ladies had they been obliging. A cook engaged from a local registry office reproved me for killing flies as 'they purified the air'; her successor smoked cigarettes and thought the ash improved the pastry. From all this jetsam and flotsam a treasure emerged at last, to be half killed on her Sunday evening out by a motor-cyclist. But the kitchen was always the Achilles Heel of the household.

Let me remember with gratitude Mrs. Meek, so suitably named, who opened my door punctually at seven, never failed with bath water at eight and bacon at eight-thirty, who despatched five children to school, washed for two families, fed four pigs, and kept one, a drunken husband on the dole, who betted and raised credit for cigarettes in her name at the grocer's. Not one of her children had a dirty face or an unstitched garment. She would not take an apple without asking, and when her rheumatism was at its worst sang loudly 'Jesu, Lover of my Soul,' not in tribute to Christian Science, but in Christian defiance. She died, suddenly, as she had lived, at the wash-tub, and, as her own night-gown was in it, a neighbour had to provide one in which to lay her out.

For six weeks she 'obliged' me, and in her case the word was correct. There followed a manservant, with little linen but ample insolence, who left after a week because it was a mile and a half to a cinema. He forgot to take a book called *Manners for Men* and a packet of letters from a girl threatening proceedings for maintenance.

Gradually, from various sources, I learned the history of my cottage. It was haunted; two people had recently died there. Since it was built in the reign of Queen Elizabeth I calculated that quite fifty persons must have died in it and many more have been born. The scenes enacted in any bedroom four hundred years old will keep the imagination busy. But the two deaths of which I was made aware were matter for romance rather than remorse in the eyes of the village.

Some years previous an elderly British Consul had cast his spell over an elderly lady in the American city where he resided. When he retired, the enamoured lady, unable to bear the separation, followed him to

England, and greatly to his embarrassment settled near
Henley, where he had chosen to end his days. If she
had one passion as great as her attachment to the retired
Consul it was her passion for the English countryside. Centuries of exile had not succeeded in suppress-
ing in her racial inheritance a nostalgia for old England. Thus two passions were conveniently united—her
desire to be near the Consul, her desire to dwell in
the English countryside. Rumour varies upon the degree of encouragement she received, when, within walking distance of the elderly beloved, she found all her
heart desired.

In the middle of a cabbage plot were two dilapidated
cottages. Something in their setting, the contour of
their crazy roofs, the warp of blackened timber and
dormer windows, filled her with the desire of possession. She bought them, and compensated the evicted
tenants. She knocked the two cottages into one, closed
up a door, put in a bath-room, added a window, and
installed the solitary radiator which had surprised us
on our first inspection. Painted, white-washed and
made weather-proof, she owned at last a cottage in
England. With what excitement that elderly widow
must have closed the door of her dwelling when she
retired on the first night, to sleep near, if not near
enough, the man she loved.

Buying and altering the cottage were only the beginning of the labour she lavished on her possession.
When my visitors nowadays are complimentary about
the garden I hasten to mention her name. It is her
best memorial, and her last years were spent in shaping
it and stocking it. She was inspired when she

wrapped the cottage round with a lawn, a border of thrift, flower-beds and a hedge, conforming to the larger concentric pattern of the hills among which it nestled. Then she hid away the matter-of-fact end of every house, the kitchen, in the dense yew. She covered the useless exterior of the bake-oven with small cypresses, and planted in one corner four poplar trees. She knew that in time they would stretch to the sky, leading the eyes to the wooded hills beyond, and dwarf and anchor the cottage at their feet. She knew how to break the line of circular hedge with hawthorn branches and wild rose.

It was she who had named the place Pilgrim Cottage. She had built the rustic porch with seats before the door, and the clematis-covered arch over the garden gate. She had planted the crimson ramblers that closed in the east end of the garden, and in the beds themselves she had gathered a varied and joyous company of flowers. Had it been her thought to train a rambler along the supported bough of an apple tree, and hide away the drainpipes at the north end of the house behind a most carefully planned screen of honey-suckle and jasmine?

Little by little I learned more of this woman who loved her garden. The villagers liked her. They agreed in the use of one word. She had dignity. It must have been almost formidable dignity considering the way in which the impression of her remained. "One look of 'er eye, sir, and you were mum," reported Mrs. Meek. It transpired she was a tall woman. This set me thinking. How came she to endure the low lintels on which I constantly cracked my head, with quick blasphemy? I enquired about this. Surely she had cracked her head also. Had she used 'language,' or did love of the Elizabethan scene extend to a sore scalp? "Oh no, sir, she allus kept 'er 'at on in the 'ouse!" was the answer.

There were other strange facts about the lady, as I discovered to my inconvenience. The cooking range did not work. I ascertained that it had never worked. The cottage seemed to have been lived in by raw vegetarians. As for the winter months, a cold June night coming fast on the heels of a hot June day caused me to light a fire in the drawing-room. Elizabethan fireplaces are lovely to look at, but difficult to live with. They are about as utilitarian to-day as would be a stage-coach on which everyone looked so jolly in the illustrations. The roaring log-fire, the wide chimney-place, the oak settle, with mine host dozing in top-boots, and a dog stretched before the blazing fire, are excellent in a frame, but the reality shatters the picture.

Waste and discomfort never seemed to trouble our ancestors. My fire would smoke, and the wide fire-place promoted a monstrous draught. When, later, I sought professional advice on the smoke problem, I learned that cottage chimneys were built to smoke, not only the inhabitants, but more essentially the bacon which hung from the ceiling to be cured. How had an American lady, born of a race and generation given pre-eminently to plumbing, steam heating, iced water and cold storage, all the adjuncts that make the American home a perfect hotel, endured the discomfort of poor cooking and incessant smoking? A steam radiator and a bath-room do not, in my view, take precedence of good cooking and smokeless living. The mystery was never solved, except that I learned she always went to bed as soon as it was dark. Did she winter in the bedroom with her radiator?

Whatever her life, her death was pleasant. She enjoyed only a few years in the garden she made. Then one warm June evening, when the long day had not wholly faded from the sky, and the white fox-gloves and blue delphiniums were still visible below her window, she said good-night to the woman who came in to 'do' for her, and went upstairs into the bedroom with the billowing ceiling and the dormer window that looked on to the noble sweep of Henley Park. In the morning she did not come down as usual, and the daily woman, going to her room, found her dead in bed.

When the Will was read it was found that she had ordered her body to be cremated and the ashes scattered over the garden. It was also found, to the delighted scandal of a hundred gossips, that she had left the freehold of the cottage, with all its contents, to the beloved retired Consul.

He forthwith took up his residence there, lived happily for a space of two years, and then died, similarly, retiring one evening and being found dead in bed the next morning. Pilgrim Cottage passed to a relation professionally engaged somewhere in East Africa. The cottage was closed until his return, when he could decide what to do with it. It was in this interval that I looked over the garden gate and coveted it.

My natural curiosity often caused me to reflect upon
the love-story woven into the history of Pilgrim
Cottage. Did the American lady pine away in un-
requited love, having crossed the Atlantic and forsaken
her homeland to find the pursued obdurate in his
refusal? Undoubtedly he was a charmer, for on
hearing of his death an unknown lady rushed down
to the cottage, to encounter another unknown lady;
and a bewildered solicitor, battling with hysterics, had
great difficulty in preserving peace.

Whatever the truth I cannot help feeling grateful to
the retired Consul. The lure of his personality
resulted in the cottage and the garden as I found them.
It would have been fitting had no one again lived in
that house or walked in that garden. In the Consul's
hands little was changed; either he felt the place was
hallowed or some feeling of remorse or veneration
caused him to leave everything intact. I found the
lady's books still on the shelves. There was furniture,
unmistakably American, which she had imported.
There was an album of press-cuttings relating to
family history, in which I learned that her father had
been a Colonel in the American Civil War. And
when, by way of paying the rent on departing from the
place, I wrote an article for an American paper,
fancifully asking who was this lady unknown to me
who had made a garden so lovely and left the touch of
her hand upon the place, I learned that she was no
lady of legend, as I had begun to think. A brother,
still surviving, wrote to me from New York, and said
he recognised the place to which his sister had retired
in her last years.

When the leaves fell, when the last gold had faded from the beechwoods, and all around me rose the smoke of pyres in my neighbours' gardens, I closed the gate for the last time. I had taken a rich harvest of apples from the trees, and through the winter months, as these came to my table, I thought of Pilgrim Cottage, closed and silent. I thought of it even in the sunshine of Cannes at Christmas. A winter of reflection told me this was the cottage I wanted, that it was in England I wished to settle. The old lady in Florida was right. A garden is the birthright of an Englishman.

But there were fluctuations in my desire. I suppose I should not be the kind of creature I am, evoking and recording the emotions of fictitious people if I were not wayward and restless. It is the penalty I must pay for hours of exaltation when the adventure of the mind transcends all else in this business of living. Those nine children of my blood—I had written nine novels at this period—had not been produced without much wear and tear of the spirit. It was in my mind to close the door of Pilgrim Cottage and in tranquillity deliver me of more children, less strenuously, with birth throes less acute.

Yet even now I was tempted. How lovely this terrace overlooking the harbour of Villefranche; how enticing the Roman sunset seen from the Pincio. The evening light in the Piazza at Venice, when the crowd parades and the upper sky is gold above the mosaics of San Marco; that room in the Rue de Berri where, from a balcony, the white vision of Montmartre smites the opal evening sky—one life is not enough, nor one place in which to spend that life.

But I put the thought from me. One's own land, one's own race, these when the zest goes and the spirit faints, or the external circumstances of finance or politics change, are the only sure inheritance. So all through a winter of voluntary exile I rejected each alien lure. I had arrived at a determination to buy that cottage.

In the early spring a letter informed me that the owner had decided to sell.

II

It was at this moment that temptation in the shape of Beverley Nichols crossed my path. Simultaneously with myself he had been seized by the country cottage mania. He had already bought his cottage and was now reduced to hysteria among seed catalogues in a thatched dwelling eighty miles from London. He was no sooner installed than he conceived a passion to found a colony, of which I was to be the first member. He declared he had found the very place for me. I must come and see it at once.

I found him completely rusticated, walking about with a bowed head under oak beams in a delightful trio of cottages knocked into one. Even then he had not quite decided up which of his three staircases to go to bed, but he took me out at once to show me where he had decided to sleep in the village churchyard. He was here for ever, he assured me. Here he would end his days—but would still keep his house in London in case——

"Which house?" I interrupted. I had memories

of his having encouraged me to purchase a house opposite his in Knightsbridge, and had barely declined an impossible lease ere I found he had sold and fled to Mayfair, and only caught up with him in Mayfair before he fled to Westminster.

"But I am really here for ever; I'm going to be buried here," he declared, waving a hand in the direction of the churchyard. "And I'm going to plant a forest there, and make a lake there. Just think how lovely it'll be for us; we can see each other just when we want, and avoid each other when we don't want, and when we're old——"

"—*and grey and full of years,*" I continued. "Yes —but what have you found for me?"

"To-morrow you'll see," he said, shaking a cock-tail. "It's the very place for you, and only across the road."

"How much is it?"

"Oh, that I don't know—it can't be much. Nothing is here. You'll adore it. It's the very place. Isn't it, Henry?"

"Well, I haven't seen it yet," said Henry, a fellow guest.

"We'll all see it to-morrow," cried my host. "We'll keep this village to ourselves!"

The morrow dawned, and after breakfast we set out to view my prospective home.

"Has it got a name?" I asked.

"Yes—it's the Hall. Isn't that grand? Won't it look well on your notepaper?" replied my friend.

It sounded too grand, and I was not encouraged by a prospect of living up to my notepaper. I am afraid I sounded ungrateful, but overwhelmed by such infectious enthusiasm I began to wonder what it really cost to live at a Hall.   Much depended on the size of the Hall.

We turned in at a drive.   Part of the wall by the large gate had fallen.   A short curving drive led through a wood.   Suddenly the Hall stood before us.

I do not remember having seen anywhere a more hideous, forbidding house.   It was faced with a wide gravel drive, and a small garden grown derelict.   The house was long, flat-faced, built of repellent concreted brick, with rows of oblong windows, and a sham Tudor door in the centre.   It would have served for a perfect example of a Victorian institution, a public lending library, a Ruskin Working Man's Club, or a Rechabites' Convalescent Home.   Actually I discovered that it was a Co-operative Society's Hostel.

"But it could be made to look nice," exclaimed my host, when a cry of horror escaped me.   "Wait until you see the inside."

At the entrance we lingered.   Three broken panes of glass in those long flat windows gave me a feeling of utter desolation.   The lawn and the garden had gone to ruin.   The fallen pier of the gate became symbolic of the heavy hand of Time.   But the interior had yet to be seen.   It might produce a magnificent surprise, a winding Gibbons staircase, a splendid entrance hall, Palladian or Wren, a library with fine book-racks, a drawing-room with a parquet floor, an Adam fireplace or an Italian plaster ceiling.   I recalled a friend who had bought an old Tudor farmhouse, and in the course of alterations had discovered a false

ceiling behind which lay another of priceless Floren-
tine workmanship.

"Look at that!" exclaimed my host, pointing to a
stone entablature over the door. It was a coat of
arms, in excellent preservation, with two deer rampant
as supporters, and a motto. "Doesn't that look fine!"

It did. I had a swift vision of the crunch of tyres on
the gravel drive, the arrival of a friend's Rolls-Royce
with a freight of lovely ladies for lunch, and myself,
not undistinguished, the local squire indeed, receiving
my guests under that flamboyant coat of arms, not my
own, though owned by me.

Another vision somewhat perturbed me, threatening
the harmony of the proposed colony. My friend was
certain to write a book about his place, as he did indeed,
successfully and brilliantly, and I was certain to write
a book about my place, as I have now done. I foresaw
carefully veiled annoyance when visitors sought our
respective shrines. I don't think any village can support two authors. The god of Fame is a jealous god.

I pictured the scene. The car-load of autograph
hunters would be heard approaching from the main
road. The owner of the Hall and the owner of the
Cottage would scurry into hiding, preparatory to
assuming that surprised annoyance which tradition
has prescribed for the Man of Fame sought out by The
People. ("Tennyson is very annoyed by the crowds
that stand at his garden gate"—"He'd be much more
annoyed if they didn't!"—Coventry Patmore to a
friend.) There would be a moment when the car
turned in at the Hall gates, or went on to the Cottage,
an almost unbearable moment for the lurking celeb-

rities. The Hall might win by magnificence, but the Cottage would have the lure of the antique, infallible with Americans. Would it not be human for the owner of the Cottage, on a tactless allusion to the occupant of the Hall, to observe that such apparent prosperity had nothing to do with 'sales,' the place was bought very cheap? And the owner of the Hall, in similar circumstances, might slyly observe that, of course, the occupant of the Cottage, who wrote so brilliantly about gardening, really knew nothing about it, and got his. . . .

This would not happen, of course. The tactful people who visited us both would effect a nice exchange of compliments. But I could not wholly dismiss possibilities of friction, and, authorship apart, there might ensue fierce competitive gardening, a coolness between us over the height of my hollyhocks or the condition of his tomatoes. There is tremendous passion burning in the subsoil of a gardener's nature.

Such were the thoughts hovering subconsciously as I passed under the coat of arms and entered the hall. This would not have distinguished even one of those contractors' 'palaces' enjoying the turmoil of an arterial road, and obtainable for one payment down with a Building Society, which never builds, but borrows and lends. Still anxious for distinction we pressed on into the drawing-room. It surpassed all expectations, in squalor. Down the inside wall of this oblong room, facing the factory windows, there was a crack of doom. At the extreme end of this room a mantelpiece of robust ugliness killed all visions of the Adam brothers, and the floor, eaten with dry rot before

the fireplace and windows, revealed the dusty founda-
tions. The fact that it would make a ball-room, as
someone observed, with new window frames, new fireplace, new floor, a renewed wall, and some kind of
lighting, for none existed, did not raise my spirits.
But undaunted, my friend led on into a commonplace
dining-room, used for Co-operative teas, and up the
plain staircase.

I remember well, during the march of the British
Armies to the Rhine, visiting a sick prisoners' hospital
when we occupied Aix-la-Chapelle. Most of the
prisoners were Russians, with a mixture of French and
English. The wards consisted of a number of barren
rooms opening off a barren corridor. In these rooms
were skeleton figures in skeleton iron beds.

I was reminded of this hospital now. This corridor,
these rooms, were as gaunt and forbidding. They
held no sick prisoners, but they seemed to have held
them. Actually, the skeleton iron beds were there,
grim reminders of vanished or deceased housemaids.

We tramped from room to room. There was not a
single feature of any charm in this wilderness of bedrooms. I had wondered about the view from the back
of the house. The front had been so forbidding that
I anticipated a back view of delightful gardens and
lovely vistas. Alas, there was no back, nothing
but a grim brick wall. Beyond were some fields, and
on the horizon a group of hideous farm servants'
dwellings.

Then, at the far end of the house, we discovered a
bath-room, entangled in lead pipes like poor Laocoön.
The kitchen and boiler were situated at the other

extremity of this barracks. Hot water had as much chance of reaching Mount Everest as this bath-room. And the poor legs of the maids, summoned through a series of swing doors along draughty corridors! But the second half of the house had been added in the early Victorian era, when the price of a servant-girl's legs was not more than four shillings a week, and a special synovitical disease known as 'housemaid's knee' was rampant. Now the disease has passed to the mistress running around Registry Offices.

It was during the close of our survey that I became aware of a pungent odour. There was an unmistakable smell of cows. A question elicited the truth. It was cows. The offices at the end of the Hall, around the yard beyond, were used as sheds for the cows on the Co-operative farm! Here they were driven twice a day for milking, passing in and out with that easy insanitary habit of cows. Amid the early morning clanging of milk churns would arise this odour, and again at even. For it transpired that an enterprising Co-operative Society in a near town had bought, as a job lot, the farm buildings, the land and the Hall. They were now willing to dispose of the Hall, and my friend had seen a splendid chance for me.

My curiosity concerning the noble former owner of the Hall was satisfied later when I visited the church. He had died some sixty years before. Misfortune seemed to have dogged this family. A viscounty and an earldom had died out, failing direct issue, and the Irish barony had been retained only by the widest jumps in the succession. The late holder's wife died abroad at an early age. He lived alone for many years at the dismal Hall, looking eagerly forward to the day when his daughter, her schooling finished, would lighten his loneliness. Then, one day, he was stunned by the news that his daughter had married. He lingered on in his loneliness, and died at the age of eighty. The title passed to the next of kin in the Colonies. The weeds grew over the Hall drive, the garden became a wilderness, the wall cracked, the floor rotted, only the coat of arms somehow kept intact, over the paintless door.

In a corner of the churchyard, under long grass and obliterating ivy, I found the resting-place of the old baron. By the irony of fate his name was misspelt in the memorial window in the church. Had the house possessed charm I think a history so dismal would have prevented my purchase. I am always acutely conscious of the atmosphere that places derive from former occupants.

My friend was in no way perturbed by my refusal to become the owner of the Hall. He saw the funny side of his proposition, and straightway produced another. It transpired that the Dower House and farm were for sale. I could still be housed in dignity in his vicinity.

We inspected the house. It was not unattractive, despite the fact that the middle dormer window, cocked askew, gave it a sinister appearance. It was built also of forbidding grey stone, but the view was delightful. I was a little alarmed to discover that the farm consisted of two hundred acres, and still more alarmed when we inspected the large barns and farm buildings. I knew something of the cost of keeping these in repair, and of hedging, gating and ditching. Moreover, I had no

intention of becoming a farmer. I had neither the
leisure, energy nor wealth for such a hobby.

But my friend airily dismissed all these obstacles;
indeed, he proved that the income from the farm, which
could be let, would give me the house free of cost. In
vain I demurred. We studied the auctioneer's Bill of
Sale, we even motored into the nearest town to interview
the agent, a solicitor of considerable charm and suavity,
who received us in an old-world atmosphere that seemed
to come straight out of the Barsetshire Chronicles.

The price being reasonable, we decided to view the
property. Here I hesitated. The Dower House was
still inhabited by the owner, a farmer who was being
compelled to sell. Poor man, I hated the idea of tramp-
ing all over his house, thrusting my nose into private
rooms, inspecting and assessing the merits and demerits
of his property. It might have a serious reaction on
his wife and children, threatened with the loss of the
old house. An imaginative man, I suffer all the appre-
hensions that may visit others affected by my action.

Steeling my nature I rang the front bell, conscious
that unfriendly eyes had followed the interloper up the
drive from the gate. A maid received us, and ushered
us into a farmer's drawing-room, always a conventional
place for no purpose except weddings, funerals and the
vicar's call. Then the mistress appeared, polite but
cool. We announced our mission, and were conducted
over the house. With every step I became more
certain it was all impossible. What should I do with
this enormous kitchen, the outbuildings, the farm?
The most attractive view called for the insertion of a
window, the plain front could be made symmetrical

with a bow window and a porch. There was probably oak under the covered ceiling. There was certainly expense at every hand. If I bought the place I should not have the heart to turn out these worthy people, smitten by the hard hand of the times. No, I did not want a farm, a farmyard, a host of barns, a farmhouse. Then, in the cellars I found a loophole of escape. The house possessed a phenomenon. It was built on a spring. There, in the very centre of the house, water welled up. There were times when it flooded the cellar.

My friend was fascinated by this 'asset' as he called it. He had to pump all his water, whereas I had it flowing under, if not over, my very doorstep. But I was not fascinated, I was alarmed. An hereditary tendency to rheumatism was my excuse. Frightened by the farm, I felt delivered by the spring. I was not destined to live at the Dower House.

Anyone less determined or ebullient than my friend would have wiped his hands of me after this. But I was not to escape from the proposed colony of desirable people. Undismayed by my rejection of the Hall and the Dower House, he had discovered something more modest, a true cottage that was for sale. When I saw it I realised we had gone from the absurd to the ridiculous, from the Hall to the hat-box. It had a living-room, two attics and an outhouse. There was no spring, there was no water of any kind. The garden was the size of a strip of carpet, the living-room was certainly antique and too full of oak beams, for the ceiling was only five and a half feet high. That was a small matter, said my friend. If you cannot raise a

ceiling then you lower a floor.   There was no view, no
garden.   But why bother with a view when you live in
the midst of them; and there was always his garden
at my disposal.   Water was obtainable in a bucket
a quarter of a mile away.   The cottage faced some
derelict labourers' dwellings.   These were shortly to
be repaired and would not then be unsightly.

I marvel still, such was the persuasive power of my
friend, that I made two journeys into the near town to
interview the owner.   But some guardian spirit caused
me to temporise even after the price was agreed.   I
went back to London, and a letter awaiting me there
concerning Pilgrim Cottage dismissed all other tempta-
tions.   Moreover, far removed from my friend's
infectious charm, I regained my balance.   It was
Pilgrim Cottage I wanted.

But Henry had fallen.   He bought the cottage.   A
year later he sold it.   When, eighteen months later, I
was again my friend's guest he showed me with great
delight an empty house.   The thatch needed repairing,
there was a derelict garden full of bottles and cans, and
by the water-butt lurked three homeless cats, the
property of the last owner, who had been taken to an
asylum.   My friend had persuaded a 'colonist' to buy
the place.   He was retiring and intended turning it into
a village store.   Wasn't it splendid, and couldn't it be
made lovely? asked my friend, making his third survey
within two days.

But looking at the wild garden, the wild cats, the
water-butt and the grim windows, my heart was heavy
within me for the new member of the colony.   When
the long winter nights closed in, the rain dripped, and

the soul craved company, in the cold loneliness the
owner of the store would receive a cheerful card from
his persuasive neighbour—basking in the sun of Egypt
or the Riviera.

III

I was quite sure now that I wanted Pilgrim Cottage.
I began negotiations, following the letter from the
agents, and after some argument we narrowed the
breach between us.   In the month of May I took part
in a small ceremony that was quite unreal to me.   In
a room on the upper floor of a dull house in Clifford
Street, where the roar of Bond Street grew faint, and
an air of ancient leisure possessed the mellowed street,
a solicitor rustled papers on his desk, asked me to sign
my name, then to put my finger on a certain spot, and
murmur like an incantation, "I deliver this as my act
and deed."   He took from me a cheque on which I
had written my name and a figure, and then, following
another shuffling, announced that Pilgrim Cottage was
mine.

I looked out of the window across the street into a
room where coatless men tailored the British officer.
In a room above a typist manicured her nails while a
young man gossiped with her.   Below, in the street, a
fashionable lady picked up a Pekinese and entered her
Rolls-Royce.   A peal of bells in the tiled tower of a
scent shop sent a Bruges-like clamour through the
London air.

All this happening around me had an air of unreality.
Even the well-groomed gentleman in front of me, pearl-
pinned and stripe-trousered, glancing at the clock with

a thought for the corner table in the Devonshire Club, hardly existed for me. A russet-tiled cottage with five dormer windows, four poplars and a well, was now mine. By this mere act of paper shuffling in a London office I had gone rustic.

ON HEARING BIRDSONG

A blackbird sang in the apple tree
And my heart leapt up, for I knew beyond doubt
That the music of Life will endure when we
Leave this World's last room, and to Time pass out
On the unknown way.   And a thought grew strong—
Since a bird sings here, and through centuries old
Sang thus for others who passed along,
Time's not a wind so terribly cold!

CHAPTER IV

A SALE IS HELD

I

THE perfect house does not exist. Men who have houses built for them quarrel with their architects. Men who inherit houses want to get rid of them. Men who buy old houses immediately set about altering them.

I in no way differ from my fellows. There was a lot required doing in the cottage. Even now there is a lot to be done. There always will be. And should the day ever come when nothing more can be done, no tile repaired, no crack sealed up, no door rehung, there will always be the garden. No man has ever finished with his garden. He must bend to it until finally the soil covers him from sight.

I bought the cottage in May and looked forward to spending the summer in a place furnished to my taste. I allowed six weeks for alterations. Being a good-natured person, I agreed that the late owner should hold a sale on the premises within a reasonable time. When the sale was over and the workmen were gone I moved into the cottage. It was the nineteenth of September. I had been robbed of another summer.

Nevertheless, I learned much in those months of agitation. The sale of furniture was held by a local auctioneer. He was much too local, for he held the sale in my garden, placing his rostrum directly over the central flower-bed. He had two heavy-footed assistants, who dragged all the furniture out of the cottage and across the bed. It seemed to me that the whole County turned up for the sale of these miserable articles. They tramped upstairs and down, poked their heads into every cupboard, and made disparaging remarks about the furniture and the late tenant. Only about three per cent. were buyers. The village seized this opportunity of penetrating the house of a woman who had kept to herself.

The chief bait seemed to be a Chippendale chair. I had passed many uneasy evenings in it. It may have been a thing of beauty, but it was never a joy to sit on. It had been cunningly glued in places and was much restored. But it was Chippendale, and the name, printed in block letters in the catalogue, went to the heads of a number of grey-haired women. They came with the light of battle in their eyes. For some unknown reason two pairs of coloured sheets, a bilious green and a revolting pink, sent them into a frenzy of possession. They paid for them just twice what new ones cost.

I bid for a pair of tapestry curtains. A woman with a neck like a plucked turkey was determined that I should not have these or any other curtains. Each time I retired defeated. At the end of the day she came and offered me all I had bid for.

"I don't really want them," she said.

"Then why did you bid against me?" I asked, annoyed.

"Oh, I don't know—but if you want them——"

"Nothing would induce me to have them, and I hope your husband likes them," I replied, exasperated.

Auctioneers thrive on feminine hysteria. I had never attended a sale before, and was astonished by all I saw. It provided me with the opening of a new novel. Dozens of friends had proudly exhibited things they had 'just picked up' at sales. Now, having attended a sale, I am very sceptical about those pickings. It seemed to me on that memorable day that a sale was something like a fire, the more rubbish you threw in the higher the blaze.

There was a terrible Sheraton screen that had almost brained me on several occasions with its contortionist tricks. The auctioneer's assistant, demonstrating its gymnastic qualities, became imprisoned in it and trapped his fingers. I was afraid that it might be left with me, unwanted and homeless, but three ladies at the back, after a long pause in which there were no bids, suddenly decided, together, that it was just the screen they had been looking for. The auctioneer hid his astonishment. In the last round between a lady whose false teeth chattered with agitation and a rival with a shooting stick, the screen was again unfolded and closed up, with resentful caution, by the assistant.

The lady who triumphed had come in a 'baby' car. She was determined to take the screen with her, the car was determined she should not. The subsequent effort reminded me of those Chinese cube puzzles that vexed us as small boys.

I had reserved my last bidding for the gardening implements. These were now necessities to me. They looked rather sad, gathered together under the apple tree. I thought of the many times their owner had toiled with them, of the years through which the old gardener, so old that he was almost Elizabethan himself, had laboured with them. A roller, a lawn-mower, various rakes, two spades, a hose, a long ladder, a small glass frame, a watering-can, a water-butt, some cane chairs, a rustic garden seat, shears of various sizes, all these things so strange to me, would now come into my life. I decided to acquire them. They were the last items in the sale. Most of the people would be gone. I should get them cheap. No one would want to go home with a garden roller.

I am still overcome by the recollection of what happened. The auctioneer left his rostrum and went over to the apple tree where the implements were gathered. Suddenly there was a wild surge, a mael-strom of humanity sweeping across the lawn, across the beds, in the wake of the auctioneer. The air was filled with the murmur of voices. I found myself shut off on the outside of that raging crowd, the auctioneer completely hidden from view.

But as I stood there I heard voices bidding, and prices offered, that made my head reel. Those miserable-looking garden tools were fetching more than the furniture! The rustic seat I had disdainfully sat on, and thought of offering seven shillings for, fetched three pounds. The ladder soared, as ladders should, far out of my reach, even had my bid been heard above the babel. As for the mower and the roller, I wondered if ever I should be able to afford either now that these were taken from me. The bidding was so brisk, the fervour so great, that the sale was over before

I had recovered from my astonishment. Even a bag of onions left over in the outhouse had been swept away in that final lust for possession.

The next day in that ruined garden I was faced by an implementless and reproachful gardener. He had no tools with which to work, and I had straightway to motor into the nearest town and buy mower and roller, and countless objects of the gardener's trade. The prices I had to pay so horrified me, and enlightened me, that a few days later I invested in the shares of a garden tools manufacturing company. In the subsequent financial crisis, these not only maintained their dividends but declared a bonus. That sale had made me aware of a lust for garden rollers.

II

It is a common lament that the aristocracy are passing from the land. The noble lord, the proud baronet, and the well-connected parson have vanished. Don't believe it. The old families have gone, it is true. Within a year of my arrival a family who had supplied the squires for a couple of centuries, and with whose name were associated as many benefactions as acres, was driven by taxation to sell land, woods and cottages and retreat to a small corner of a once splendid domain. The change, as always, was for the worse. Land sharks and property profiteers stepped in, the old cottagers trembled for the roofs above them, and heartless speculators wrought havoc in magnificent woodlands, where the axe of the feller devastated hillsides and valleys as noble as any in this English scene.

Contrary to belief, there is no dearth of aristocracy on the land, but it has retreated to the dower house or the cottage, and is swamped by the new-rich whose limousines crackle up the gravel drive, where once a pair of spanking horses clattered with a jingle of harness. Let it be said that some of the newcomers behave worthily. They acquire titles to impress their neighbours, they play the grand seigneur to the village at their gates, they make the cottages sanitary, they turn barns into ball-rooms and music-rooms. They brighten the lives of a brood of close-living gentlefolk with lavish hospitality, with tea parties, tennis parties, dinners and dances.

Old Miss Arabella Mervyn-Morpeth, the grand-daughter of a dead Admiral, in Debrett by virtue of a deceased mother who was an Honourable, is inclined to sniff and rub in the Admiral, of whom a gouty painting dominates the drawing-room at Page's Bottom (this district abounds in Bottoms belonging to owners who were variously named Bix, Fawley, Hogendon, Oxlands, Bromsden, Pinewell and Spratt). But sniff-ing she goes, and smiling she leaves. She came on foot, she departs on air cushions, for Lord Bowerdale has pity on her old feet and stiff back, and sends her home in one of his five cars.

Lord Bowerdale, who started life in overalls and is ending it in ermine, is always helping someone, from a sly gift for the parson's son at Oxford, down to a cartload of manure for a rose-growing tenant. The Bowerdales bring their money from the factories where they have made it, and apply it to dignifying themselves and their surroundings. I prefer them to

the retired shopkeeper who parades his overdressed
family in a large car, and plasters the grounds of
Chatsworth with 'Trespassers Will Be Prosecuted.'

My terrain, I was soon to discover, is planted thick
with the new aristocracy, but here and there the Old
Guard stand by tradition. They are gracious, they
take tea with parvenus, go to the garden-parties of
social climbers, and trade somewhat on the renown of
being *persona grata* at Court. They are the only
remaining people for whom the tradesman comes to
the door of his shop. They have faded from bazaars,
where others are more lavish, and from flower shows,
where they cannot compete with establishments with
ten gardeners. But they are firmly to the front when
Royalty is in the neighbourhood.

I do not know why snobbery is so venomously
denounced. Surely it is the most harmless of social
vices? The doctor's wife who is made happy by
having a Marchioness to lunch is probably ambitious
for her husband's practice. Love of the poor and
lowly is not necessarily associated with a yearning for
their company, and in my experience Socialists are
the least sociable of people, and have a fine scorn
for all who have not seen the Light of their very
plain day.

When I hear people complain that the fount of
honours plays too lavishly, I retort that it cannot
sprinkle too many. Let us all have ermine and straw-
berry leaves, garters, collars, ribbons and stars. All the
world's a stage, and I'm all for a well-dressed pageant
so long as we don't take it too seriously. Nations
that abolish this pleasant make-believe generally take

to hangings and shootings in their serious moods of brotherhood and equality.

It was wrong, of course, that in our village life the squire and the vicar should have lived in the only decent houses and thrived in leisure, while around them a horde of illiterate boors spent their lives bowed to the soil. Revenge has been taken for this state of things, and a revolution in the kitchens of large houses has caused distress in their drawing-rooms. But we have learned in these last few years that equality has little to do with happiness, and the struggle for existence in the bed-sitting-rooms of the West End, conditioned by an artificial-silk civilisation, and an artificial-food nutrition, is just as severe in nervous taxation, and far more impoverished in tranquillity, than anything known to the country clod.

Enough of this contemplation of the social scheme. My cottage, for many centuries the scene of life's incessant circle, birth, marriage and death, required attention. Furtive courtships, clumsy seductions and rush-lighted quarrels and feastings, all these had been encompassed in conditions of penury and discomfort. What would the Elizabethan, Carolinian and Georgian ghosts make of this place carpeted and curtained, with radiators and hot and cold water in all the bedrooms, with a car in the garage, capable of seventy miles an hour on the road, a telephone on the table capable of ten thousand miles a second through the air, with visitors calling from London one hour distant, and opera pouring in from Rome, Milan, Prague and Stuttgart at the mere turn of a button?

There was a night when my secretary swore a ghost

was tapping the typewriter downstairs. Actually it proved to be impatient birds pecking at the empty bird-table below the window, but for a few moments I played with the idea of a contemporary Shakespeare's answering a letter from Sir Walter Raleigh:

"With reference to yours of the 9th inst., *re* a consignment of Virginian Tobacco delivered at Plymouth . . ."

Upset the sequence of Time, provide Pericles with a Maxim gun and Cromwell with a telephone, and history would have to be re-written. Every time the telephone rings in my sixteenth-century drawing-room I am aware of the fantastic incongruity of that summons through space. "That you, Cecil? Richard speaking. Just heard that Drake defeated the Spanish Armada this afternoon—thought you'd like to know."

But the telephone is not yet in the house, nor the radiators, nor the radio. The car lacks a garage, the kitchen a pantry. Doors must be raised, partitions must come down, walls must be stripped, brickwork painted. One bold innovation I have already planned. The cold, unwanted dairy, sunk into the earth under that long sweeping roof, will be converted into a housekeeper's bedroom. She will then have her own suite intact on one level. For this purpose the dairy floor must be raised to the kitchen level, and a window, cunningly matched with its fellow dormers, let into the roof. Already I have earmarked some tiles on a derelict barn for this purpose.

I have said my district was well supplied with County stock. A plentiful growth of lords and ladies was accompanied by a goodly crop of baronets and

knights. The leaves of Debrett covered many rustic
retreats, and the landscape was rich with the arbours
of peers, beds of baronets and pleasances of parvenus.
Happily I was remote enough not to be dazed by this
brilliance, though it did happen that my housekeeper
was reproved for coveting forbidden fruit—"Those
bananas are reserved for his lordship," said the shopkeeper. Was it a rumour of that reproof, reaching his
lordship's ears, that resulted in the present of a brace
of partridge?

Nearer to me, not shut off by a reservation of bananas, dwelt a baronet, albeit an Irish one with an enterprising wife. This cheerful and industrious lady
possessed after her name the most formidable array of
letters I have ever encountered, an abracadabra, I
learnt later, denoting pre-eminence in the poultry
world, and frightening familiarity with Wyandottes,
Buff Orpingtons and Plymouth Rocks. Strange that
these last should be connected by name with the
Mayflower Puritans, whose marital habits surely bore
no resemblance, despite the fecundity proven by the
millions of Americans claiming descent from those
sturdy breeders.

Lady Buff Orpington (shall we say) was renowned in
one other sphere. She had a genius for conversion,
not of the Stock Exchange variety which leads to glory
or the gaol, but of cottages almost derelict. Under
her magic touch tumbling barns and ruined roofs were
converted into alluring dwellings, and, where rags and
cobwebs had covered shattered panes, bright chintz
curtains now hung in the windows of unrecognisable
cottages.

Nothing was too derelict, too ugly for her persuasive hand. Her 'before' and 'after' photographs surpassed anything produced by the face-lifter or hair-grower. Certainly her skilful energy brought back to health many a falling cottage, and preserved for us a little longer the thoughtless beauty of the Elizabethan builder. It is true her hobby had its remunerative aspect, though in my case kindness and enthusiasm were her sole motives. By a fortunate chance I obtained her intelligent co-operation at the outset. An old shed was converted into a garage with such skill that the life of a threatened poplar tree was spared, and from the exterior no one could say where the sixteenth century ended and the twentieth began.

Kitchen larders do not sound attractive things. Little versed as I was in such a domestic matter, I realised the importance of keeping cool. Having sacrificed a dairy for the comfort of a housekeeper, how should I keep the butter firm and prevent the milk from turning? One of the features of Pilgrim Cottage was that it had no kitchen-end, no forbidding area of lavatory and coalhouse. Even the tradesmen's 'entrance' was via a pleasant south window. The essential external pipes of the house and the domestic chimney were hidden by the yew. This blank end of the house was cloaked by an arbour covered with honeysuckle and jasmin.

It was here that my collaborator ingeniously built a larder. She knocked a hole through the kitchen wall, built out a kind of box with metal network sides, and scooped out a hole in the earth which she cemented and slated to act as a cooling pit. I had the gravest doubts about the efficiency of this simple arrangement. Could food be kept fresh by a mere draught; would that earth-box preserve a low temperature through the heat of summer? To-day, when I produce in the midst of June a bottle of ice-cold hock, and the blancmange preserves the mould of fashion through the hottest noon, I feel ashamed of my scepticism. Lady Buff Orpington knew her business far better than a renowned architect, who, up at the Hall, planned a kitchen larder next to the boiler-house!

The workmen entered the house in June. They were scheduled to leave it at the end of the month. Warned by the experience of others, I arranged to move in at the end of July. In the middle of August the carpenter's bench stood in the drawing-room amid a delicious smell of shavings. Upstairs the plumbers and the painters were contesting for right of way. In vain I protested and spoke of breach of contract. The summer was slipping away, the cost was mounting up. Doubtless I was tiresome. I had all the door lintels heightened upstairs and down, determined to save my scalp. The scalping mania seems to have descended to modern sanitary engineers, who place shelves over wash-basins, nicely calculated to brain one in the act of rinsing.

Pipes of radiators running down a wall are usually placed where the light strikes them. The walls of old houses cannot be penetrated where one wishes, and solid floors prohibit under-running. I covered up the pipes in my drawing-room with a dummy beam, and encased a wall-radiator, hung to ensure a flow back, in book-shelves. My carpenter was an artist, more devoted because at that moment he was reading a serial from my pen in his daily newspaper. Authorship has its rewards in unexpected quarters.

Thus June went, and July. In August they were still making mortar on the lawn and shavings in the drawing-room. I knew then I had been robbed of a summer. Doubtless my fussy presence was a cause of irritation. Once when my car drew up I heard a voice exclaim through the garage roof, "Gawd, that bloke's here again!"

So I went off on a walking tour along the Rhine, and looking down one night upon the moonlit river thought of the silence in my English garden, and the deep shadow of a gable on the lawn. Then, early in September, excited with expectancy, I came home and rushed to Pilgrim Cottage. The workmen were still there. It seemed to me they would be there a year later; they had grown to like the place. I sent them all packing. A smell of paint pervaded the rooms. Nevertheless, I went to the local telephone and ordered the furniture to be moved in. The next day the van arrived. At eleven o'clock at night, dirty, exhausted and excited, when Mrs. Meek had gone home, Louis Tissier, my secretary, bolted the door and uncorked a bottle of Rüdesheimer. Solemnly we toasted Pilgrim Cottage. It was the nineteenth of September.

Then we went up to bed.

THE YOUNG MOON

With passionless and gentle grace
   The young Moon sees her bridegroom, Night,
And there is wonder in her face
   Which grows the purer in his sight,
Until the starry bridesmaids, crowding,
   Shine more splendid in her train,
And wish her joy no moment's clouding,
   No tears her radiant face to stain.

CHAPTER V

SOME TIPS FROM TILLY

I

I WAS inclined at first to lament that the garden was only a quarter of an acre. It looked small, I could almost see all round it at a glance. And quite one half of this area was grass. Most Newlyweds, seeking their first home, find a house with a tiny garden, and often they reject a place that suits them because the garden seems too small. Finally, they take a house with an acre or two. There is much feverish digging, much bold and alarming expenditure. Nurseries are visited, shoots and cuttings from friends are gratefully accepted, and, inevitably, a little harmless thieving is done. "Oh, they'll never miss it!" says Mrs. Newlywed, darting down and scooping out with her fingers a little plant in the garden of a house to let. The fact that she has ruined a manicure that cost five shillings for a plant not worth sixpence never occurs to her.

There is a shameful plant that I filched from a property for sale. It ought to have died, but it flourishes. I regard it with a fondness above all other blooms. Ten years of Scripture lessons were unavailing against that bright temptation. The Newlyweds have stocked their garden from various sources. John has been made to stop the car, even on the incline, to dig up those wild violets. He has been sent across London to buy packets of seeds.

Which are the greatest liars, railway posters with their sub-tropical scenes of English seaside resorts, or seed packets with their illustrations of unbelievable growth and brightness? Those palm-fringed promenades by an azure sea dotted with yachts, so often drizzle-doomed vistas of concrete and grey water, with never-green bushes between shelters for the retired and conveniences for the retiring, were they ever as the artist drew them? Did he fulfil his commission in a coke-heated Chelsea studio, from post-card memories of ten days in Lugano?

It can be said for seed, unlike seaside, advertisements, that on occasions they fulfil all expectations. I shall never forget the astonishment aroused by a twopenny packet labelled 'Californian Poppies.' The dry rattle of those minute seeds, mere pinheads, mocked the flaming picture on the packet. I was suspicious of poppies —were they not the reproach of the lazy farmer, and gaudy creatures of a single day?

One March day I dug a trench nine inches deep and sowed the seeds. I waited a month, watched daily and went indoors disgusted. No more twopenny packets, I vowed. Then Louis suggested that perhaps they wanted manure. I began to ask about manure, and learned that, after guano, the horse provided the best. For a week I carefully inspected the road by my dwelling, but the only deposit there seemed to be was oil from motor-cars. A herd of goats pastured on the common gave me sudden hopes, but I never succeeded in finding any contribution from those goats. They fill me with wonder now whenever I drive past them.

I was just about to interview a farmer reputed to possess one horse, or to purchase a London fertiliser of unspeakable origin, when a smart coupé drew up at my door, and a very bright young lady stepped from it. Her face is so well known that it is tiresome to go out with her. In restaurants all the people turn. She is not alone even in a swimming-pool, for all the young men pay round her like dolphins. She is pretty and witty and famous. She escaped from a Belgian convent, went on the stage unknown to her parents, and after ten years' hard work found fame on the films. She makes monstrous sums of money, such as only stockbrokers, leading lawyers and directors of Woolworth's can earn.

It says much for her charming nature that she is still surprised at her good fortune. She arrives in a new car and says, "Look—it belongs to me!" And it really does. It hasn't been lent by a car company for a photograph in *The Tatler*. She slips her thin white fingers under a rope of pearls and whispers, "They're mine —they're real!" She appears at a dinner-party in a delicious frock, and comes up to one for admiration, and says, "It's terribly expensive—I hope it looks like it!" She sounds ostentatious and Hollywood, but she isn't at all. She enjoys being an enormous success, and likes others to enjoy it also.

Years ago, when we were very poor and ambitious and had adjacent bed-sitting-rooms in Baker Street, we used to borrow shillings from each other for the gas meter. I used to read long poems to her, of my own

composition, and she never failed to show the most
convincing appreciation, which proved what a fine
actress she was even then. In return I listened while
she repeated her parts. Her memory was prodigious.
She would read a page three times and then repeat it
word perfect.

Then we lost sight of each other until one day I
received a clipping of a review of one of my books.
On the other side was the portrait of an actress who had
taken Hollywood by storm. It was my old friend. I
cabled my congratulations from New York, and a month
later we met there. She was just the same, and we sat
up till three, comparing notes. The next day she went
back to Los Angeles and I went south to Florida. Now
she stood at my garden gate. I did not even know she
was in England again.

"You do look funny!" was her first remark. "What
makes you do it?"

"Do what?"

"This simple life stuff. You don't really like it!"

"Of course I do," I answered, a little annoyed.

"But you know nothing about gardening, do
you?"

"That doesn't prevent one living in the country," I
retorted. "And how did you find me—where've you
come from?"

"What a lovely spot!" she said, ignoring my question, and walking down the path. "It was so funny.
I picked up the *Sketch*, and there you were, with a hoe
in your hand. Do you ever hoe?"

"Of course I do—I seem never to be doing anything else!"

"Well, how-d'you-do, and all that!   Now show me round, and tell me all about it."

I showed her round, and she told me all about it. I was stunned.   She knew the name of every plant, when everything came up, the soil it liked, the dressing it wanted.   She used strange words like 'trenching' and 'mulching,' she spoke of 'composts.'   She paused in front of the leafless vine.   I had asked my gardener twice if it was alive, so withered and dry did it look on that south wall.

"Why don't you strip it?" asked Tilly (that's what we'll call her).

"Strip it—but it's stripped, there's not a leaf on it," I said.

"No, idiot, look—strip it, so!" she replied, and stepping over the bed of carnations pulled off a glove and began to peel the dead fibre on the branches.   To my astonishment she uncovered some dark shiny wood beneath.

"You should have cut these laterals back to one bud —give me your secateurs."

I stared at Tilly, and it wasn't her heavily kohled lashes I was staring at, or her plucked eyebrows.

"Secateurs?" I repeated bewildered.

"Heavens, you don't know what secateurs are!   Clippers for pruning.   Haven't you any?"

"No, I'll get some," I confessed, deeply humiliated.

"Then lend me a penknife."

Brought up in the belief that any woman with a penknife is a danger to herself, I lent her mine reluctantly.   She placed a thumb with a rouged nail firmly on the branch, the knife underneath and pruned it.

"When the grapes come——" she began.

"They won't come!" I retorted, derisively.

"Yes, they will.   You must thin out the bunches with some grape-thinning scissors, and on no account must you touch them.   Hold them with a forked stick, and when the berries start filling put muslin bags over them to keep the birds off."

"Tilly, my dear, you're romancing.   You can only grow grapes in hot-houses!" I protested.

Tilly looked at me with scorn.

"Don't you know that years ago there was a considerable wine industry here, from local vines?"

"No—it must have been before Cæsar came," I said, satirically.

"It was Cæsar who brought the vines," answered Tilly.   "If you can't grow these grapes for eating, then you can make wine of them.   I'll give you the recipe, remind me."

All this was in early March.   In September I found she had not lied.

But we are still in the garden with Tilly.

"Your apple trees want pruning," she said, walking round the lawn with me.   "And the montbretia's killing the ramblers."

She pointed to some small green blades, so small and thin that their chance of killing the sturdy ramblers covering my fencing seemed quite absurd.   I said so, politely, whereupon Tilly demanded a trowel.   I produced one.   She squatted down and commenced digging.   Then to my amazement she plunged her delicate hands into the wet soil and began groping. When her hands emerged they were full of small bulbs.

"What did I tell you? These bulbs are choking the rambler roots, that's why so many have died off. Take out all those montbretias. Don't let them get near a rambler, they're thugs."

Then, in the same breath, she demanded, inconsistently:

"What are they—*Lord Nelsons* or *Lady Hamiltons*, or *Etoiles de Feu?*"

"Lord Nelson, Lady Hamilton," I repeated, my eyes closing in enchantment. "Do they come from Naples or from Mont Bretia, and how shall I tell the bold Admiral from the Bacchante?"

"*Lord Nelson's* scarlet and *Lady Hamilton's* apricot. There's also *Etoile de Feu*, which is orange, oh—and *Drop d'Or*, which is yellow."

"I'm all for a liaison of *Lord Nelson* with *Lady Hamilton*," I said, rubbing those oniony bulbs in the palm of my hand. "Where can I play pander with them?"

"Anywhere, they're hardy," said Tilly, waving the trowel. At that moment she sighted two barren beds.

"What are you doing with those?" she asked.

"I've done it, and nothing's happened. I've sowed poppies."

I did not then know their history, how they were loved in the gardens of ancient Rome. Three kinds were popular—white, black and red. The seeds of the white poppy were used in cooking. The Romans glazed their bread with the yolk of an egg and sprinkled the seeds on the top for decoration and taste. The tradition endures to this day, and I have bought such bread in Berlin and Rome. The juice of the black poppy was highly prized as a narcotic, and the red poppy was part of Roman history itself. When ambassadors came to Tarquin the Proud for advice how to quell the Gabians, he took them into his garden, and without making any answer, lopped off the heads of the highest poppies. Taught by this bloody symbol, the ambassadors departed, to lop off the heads of the most prominent Gabians.

The picture on the packet of Californian Poppies had excited me. I decided to buy two more packets and have a show of these gorgeous blooms. But the idea seemed to fill Tilly with horror.

"Poppies—poppies!" she exclaimed. "Why poppies?"

"Californian Poppies. They look magnificent on the packet. I put them well in, and yet nothing's happened."

"How well in did you put them—have the birds had them?"

"I don't think so," I answered. "I put them in quite nine inches."

Tilly broke into loud laughter.

"You'd better go and look for them in New Zealand —they might come up that way Don't you know that an inch or so's ample for seeds?"

"What shall I do?"

"You'd better sow some more; you won't see those."

Alas, she was wrong, quite wrong, for the next day I had a bright idea. I raked the ground over before sowing some more. I am still baffled by the result. All through the following summer I was pulling up poppies. They leapt up over night, and still more strange they leapt up all over the beds. I cannot possibly have raked up seeds nine inches deep, yet how came it that seeds appeared in places where I had never sowed them?

I asked my gardener, and got no help. He always contrived to make a deep mystery of everything. His favourite expression, in all circumstances, was "Sometimes they do, and sometimes they don't. You can't tell on our job." He was so old-fashioned that I sometimes wondered whether I hadn't acquired an Elizabethan gardener with an Elizabethan house. Yet he had no reverence for the place. "Don't understand rich folks as want to live in these Eliza-between houses," he growled. "They're all wood and worms."

Let me confess I was afraid of my gardener. I knew that he regarded me as an interloper. "It's somethink crool the way rich London folks come here and turn hardworking men out of their cottages," he exclaimed. Obviously this was one for me, though I was not rich and had the utmost difficulty in finding a hardworking man in any cottage. But I had some sympathy with him. This conversion business was changing the countryside.

Generally the conversion resulted in an improvement of the property at the cost of picturesqueness. I had discovered in my walks some abominable growths bearing abominable names, and surely inhabited by abominable people; that horror, for instance, of corrugated iron, glass and execrable chintz curtains. It was called Runnymede, and exuded

jazz music at every window. Women in trousers
leaned out smoking cigarettes, or called on motor-cycles
for a 'quick one' at the nearest inn. Happily such
examples of liberty, if not licence, were safely remote.

But I live in fear, these days of Building Societies.
Anything can happen suddenly on one's skyline. I
got up one morning and looked out of my window to
find, up by the plantation of larches that dashes itself
against the sky, a frightful thing that looked like a
monstrous yellow toadstool. I bolted my breakfast and
ascended the hill to investigate. It was not what I
feared, a permanent excrescence on the face of the
beautiful hill. It was that strange attachment to motor-
cars known as a trailer, a kind of portable bed-sitting-
room, with no proper bed and nowhere to sit, but with
art-cretonned windows and the name Carefree over
the door.

A large and expensive motor-car had towed it to the
crest of the hill and through the woods. Four people
were having a mid-morning meal, so I presumed four
people had somehow slept, or passed the night, in that
lath and canvas trailer. For me a picnic is a thing
that is delightful when it only happens once. As a
habit this portmanteau life is sheer discomfort.

I always wonder at these people who can afford high-
powered cars and expensive trailers. A wife seems
an essential part of the economy, a cook-housekeeper-
scullery-maid, who spends the morning 'buying in,'
the afternoon 'washing up,' and the evening 'going
out,' with intervals of stove lighting, water carrying
and insect fighting. Still, as the Greek philosopher

observed, 'for those who like that sort of thing that is the sort of thing they like.' It seems to me the hobby of a rich and ruthless man married to a domesticated and docile woman.

Quite frankly I am a sybarite. One is much nearer to the simple life living at the Ritz and touching a bell than lying like sardines, cooking meals and avoiding cow-pats. Ever since Jean Jacques Rousseau started the Back to Nature movement, and persuaded Marie Antoinette to wear a garland of flowers, and the ladies of the Court to look ridiculous attired as shepherdesses, who hated the smell of sheep, there has been a fashionable idea that the farther one is from comfort the nearer one is to Pan. The *reductio ad absurdum* of this movement was achived in the recent photograph of a society girl, endowed with the freedom of all the night clubs, embracing an indifferent cow as they lay in a lush landscape.

I have some right to speak of the simple life. I have walked across two continents with only a rucksack on my back, but I did not do it from choice, but because in those days insatiable curiosity outran income. Very recently, in a reaction from Lido laziness, I got out of the train at Göschenen and walked down the St. Gothard Pass to Lucerne. I had swept through that magnificent scenery so often that I was determined to see it properly, and there is only one way to see anything properly, on foot. Science, with train, car and aeroplane, only serves to telescope scenery into a kinematic procession.

As for the simple life, no one has ever reduced it to greater simplicity than those three happy German boys, Otto, Werner and Carlheintz, whom I encountered walking down the Pass. Bronzed with the sun, attired only in sandals and leather shorts, they had walked from Heidelberg, where they were students, to Venice. They were now on their way home. The whole pilgrimage of six weeks had been undertaken on a common fund of twelve pounds, and they hoped to have something left! Otto had a guitar slung on his back and the trio sang like Chinese nightingales, with a repertoire in French, Italian and English. They passed readily from *Giovanezza* to *Clementina,* and sang ballads from Heine and the Swedish that haunt me yet. They had a quick eye for scenery, but a quicker for 'a nice place to sleep in,' and I discovered that their enthusiasm for Venice was mitigated by the fact that, in a city of pavements and canals, they had been compelled to pay three lire a night for beds, and had slept uneasily.

II

Let us return to Tilly, still in the garden dispensing knowledge.

"Your lawn is lovely," she was kind enough to say. "It must have been here for years, it's quite in the Oxford tradition."

At once I exulted. I had caught her out.

"Actually, my dear, it's not been here ten years."

"What?" cried Tilly. "Impossible!"

"Wait a moment and I'll show you," I said, and disappeared indoors.

I emerged with a photograph. It had been sent to

me by a kind stranger. The photograph was of the cottage, and yet it was not of the cottage. It showed a tumbled-down place, without chimney-pots on the stacks, with a door that no longer existed on the east side. At the door was a woman in a farm bonnet, and two children. The garden in front of the door consisted of a cabbage patch, a potato plot and a rubbish dump.

"Where's this?" asked Tilly.

"Here."

"Here? Nonsense!" she retorted.

"I assure you it is. This photograph was taken just before the American descended on Pilgrim Cottage. These are the last rustic inhabitants. They survived the Great War, but they didn't survive her. She evicted them, with compensation. You're now standing on the site of the cabbage patch. The vine covers the blocked-in door."

Tilly looked at the lawn, pressed her delicate foot into it.

"It's unbelievable! They tell you at Oxford those college lawns have taken three hundred years to bring to perfection."

"It's a nice legend. I think they're very much as they were ten years after they were first laid down," I said. "Have you ever seen the lawns in front of the Trocadero in Paris? They're not fifty years old, and better than anything you've ever seen at Oxford and Cambridge. It's the juxtaposition with the buildings that makes the impression."

"I don't agree. The Trocadero lawns aren't fine," declared Tilly, with firm patriotism, "and anyhow, they're Japanese grass. What's the secret of this, fertilisers, lawn sand?"

"Neither. It's a long story, but you're in it."

"Me—what do you mean?" asked Tilly.

"Once upon a time there was a lame old man who lived in a room in a back street in London. He had a garden, but it was quite unlike all other gardens in that district. True, it had black walls with anti-catmortar——"

"With what?"

"Anti-catmortar—that was a Victorian trick, broken beer bottles stuck into mortar to stop cats walking. There were creepers that wouldn't creep, so sick were they, and bound up with cloth bandages nailed to the wall. But unique among all those back gardens, where no flowers bloomed and no washing whitened, it had a lawn of a greenness and perfection that defied all cats and chimney-pots. It literally flamed in a wilderness of windows and lace curtains. No flowers grew there, there was nothing but grass, grass so clipped, so level, so green, that when I looked out of my window——"

"Why, I remember it," interrupted Tilly, "it was at the back of our rooms. It belonged to an old man who used to sit on it in a deck-chair placed on a small carpet. It was a wonderful lawn!"

"I got to know that old man. He was taking in his bottle of milk one morning as I passed. His newspaper blew out in the draught, and I rescued it. That began our acquaintance. He was an old Indian Army officer, a widower, living in a ground bed-sitting-room with the possession of the garden. I discovered he had three passions in his life. His lawn, a log fire and Lloyd George. He liked to put a log on the fire and talk about the thing he most cherished and the person he most loathed. I once asked him how he kept his grass in such wonderful order, but I saw at once that he had a secret to preserve. After that I never bothered him again, but one day it slipped out inadvertently. I caught him shovelling the wood ash from his fire into a linen bag, and asked him why he saved it. He looked at me for a long moment and then said, 'I put it on the lawn—that's why I don't burn coal. It's the finest lawn dressing in the world.' That old man was right. Every week throughout the winter my wood ash goes on this lawn."

That, of course, is not the whole story of a good lawn. Cutting, rolling, and weeding are incessant duties. Towards the end of the summer I noticed that there was a brown circle of turf under each tree. This was due to the fact that the leaves of the trees deprived the lawn underneath of the nightly dewfall. Ten minutes' extra with the hose corrected this deficiency, and there were no yellow circuses disfiguring the emerald sward.

The small irritations of life are more wearing than the major troubles. Why do we go on using those elegant silver sugar castors that scatter their contents over the sweet and half the table? They should have gone the way of Venetian blinds (unknown in Venice) long ago. The pen that will not write, the knife that will not cut, the door that will hang open, the letter-box that tears letters, the coal scuttle that tilts over, the drawer that won't draw, the lock that won't lock, all these things wear the nerves as much as one's neighbour's radio.

To the gardener there is nothing more exasperating than a hose that just isn't long enough. For a year I suffered in this fashion. If I went round the garden to the left I just couldn't reach the bed of pinks. If I went round the garden to the right I just couldn't reach the rose-tree. The miles one walked like a surveyor's apprentice, manœuvring that hose! My garden runs round the house, my hose run round three-quarters of it. There came an evening of disaster, the stretched hose having cropped off a dozen gladioli, when I decided that, in order of necessity, a longer hose took precedence of new linoleum in the dining-room.

So I measured a complete circuit of my garden. I did more, I measured the distance beyond this, through the garage, out to the road, so that the car could be washed and the dust laid. That new hose cost me five pounds. You can do a lot with five pounds. You can start furnishing a house on the instalment plan, fly to Paris, file a divorce petition, insure your life, ascend the Matterhorn with two guides, rent an island in the Adriatic for a whole month, and buy a plot, with ten orange trees, in Florida, but none of these things will give you, a gardener, as much pleasure as an adequate hosepipe.

Every inch of mine gave me pleasure. I could walk any way I liked in my garden, the hose reeling off with obliging alacrity. My gardener became a proud man, and would walk out into the road with it on the slightest provocation. But on one occasion a passing milkman protested against being watered, which we both thought singular on the part of a milkman, since—

> *Little drops of water,*
> *Little drops of milk,*
> *Make the milkman's daughter*
> *Dress herself in silk.*

PRAYER FOR AN OLD GARDENER

Lord God of Gardens,
If you please,
Allow old Reuben
Pace his ease:
The lawns are swept,
The apples stored,
New beds are made;
But one, O Lord,
He wishes for himself to keep,
And lie there in unbroken sleep.

For eighty years
He's risen early
To tend the things
He's loved so dearly.
Spring, Summer, Autumn,
Winter, never
Escaped an eye
And hand so clever
With plants there in the potting-shed;
But now he wants to lie a-bed.

"I'm tired," he said,
"And plants keep growing,
And proper gardeners
Must keep hoeing,
My back aches awful,
My poor old knees
Give way beneath me."
So Lord, please,
Allow old Reuben Pace to sleep
Blind to the weeds that o'er him creep.

CHAPTER VI

WISE BIRDS

I

It is the common complaint of authors that publishers are too modest: they will not advertise. Sweet are the uses of advertisement, but not always. In a careless moment I had given the name of my cottage to a novel, relying upon the obscurity of both to leave me unmolested. But it was not to be. The cheerful publisher whose duty it is to assume that I am the world's greatest and best-loved author, an assumption admirably displayed in turn to the rest of his team, conceived the bright idea of making a model of my cottage, and exhibiting it in Messrs. Harrod's window as the source of the inspiration of *Pilgrim Cottage*.

At the moment I did not foresee that enthusiasm would run to such large proportions. One day a car drew up at my garden gate, and from it descended a host of designers, surveyors, photographers. They meassured, took colours, and photographed details. After an industrious day they disappeared, and I forgot all about them.

A fortnight later, arriving at Harrod's for an engagement, I stepped out of my taxi to find before me, with door open, porch clematis-covered, roses growing, and garden all in flower, my own cottage. Was I really in Knightsbridge or the Chilterns? Only the plate-glass window prevented me from walking into the cottage suddenly blooming in the middle of the Brompton Road.

The size and verisimilitude of it were breath-taking. I dare not stand and look at it. I felt suddenly shy, and hurried on. I might have heard things the crowd before the window was saying. They were possibly nice things, it looked so fresh and enticing in the hot June afternoon, amid the fumes and traffic of the London street. But I felt like a mother who sees her baby exposed at a Welfare exhibition, a little overcome, a little outraged though proud. I have never been a mother, but I assume that is how a mother does feel.

So I hurried on into the enticing maze of Harrod's. A week later, passing the window, I looked furtively. There was not much to be seen of the model; a crowd obscured it from view. "They're taking it to America," said a voice in front of me. "Some millionaire's bought it, and's going to rebuild it. This is only the model." For a moment panic seized me at the thought, but another voice distracted me—"Oh, I'd love to live in it, if only for a week."

The voice was tired, so dull with fatigue that I glanced at the speaker. She was a middle-aged woman, neatly shabby, holding a string bag. Her face was sallow and her eyes were puffy. She may have had a husband that drank or kept a fish shop in Bermondsey. Some flowers in her hat were as faded and drooping as their owner. The companion to whom she spoke was a withered little woman of her own age, monstrously gay in a lemon-coloured blouse that threw a bilious hue on her sagging face. She gripped a dwarf parasol, a mockery of elegance, in a housework-shiny hand.

At a glance I knew their courageous kind. They had formed a large part of my constituency in those days when I had to pretend to love everybody in the degrading trickery of vote-catching. In their lives a shilling had always mattered, and each day was a procession of dishes to wash, children to dress, and a scrape for the weekly insurance money that was to bury them decently. I know and respect these doughty fighters through the long littleness of life. I have drunk tea in their parlours and heard how Mr. Smith " 's 'ad nothink for a year now, 'an 'e gets very low like."

The woman with the parasol did not speak for a moment. Her eyes were busy exploring the window. Then, half to herself, she said—"Yes, I'd just like to sit in that cottage and listen to things grow. I did when I was a kid, and 'adn't the sense to know I was lucky."

'Listen to things grow.' What a phrase from that commonplace creature! It was like seeing a bed of tulips open above the stone pavement. I watched them move away, with that tired amble of kitchen-bound women. And in that odd moment, stationary on the edge of the crowd, I realised how really fortunate I was. At no moment had life been easy for me, my external circumstances until manhood had occasioned continuous anxiety. But at least in the battle I had won some slight security. Independence had been reached, and the balm of achievement helped to efface some of the bitterness of past years. By virtue of a pen I had won a passport to interesting society, to travel, to labour without coercion, to rest at will. I lived in pleasant places, observed the pageant of life, and now of my own choosing I had a quiet corner of the earth in which to dream.

All this was mine, and all this was taken for granted. These two poor women, scarred veterans in a battle with no certain issue of triumph or defeat, but only of dreary continuity, had suddenly shamed me by the smallness of their ambition. They only craved a short space in which to hear things grow.

A swift impulse stirred me. I looked for them, but they were gone. I hurried along the street wondering how I should word my surprising invitation. I would have to make them believe that I was not a madman, that I really was the owner of the original of that model, and that I really was offering them a week's hospitality, a week's retreat in which they could hear things grow. It would be something in the nature of a fairy tale to them. I felt in that moment something of the vanity of being a fairy prince. I could wave a wand, and whisk two tired women out of a wilderness of brick into an oasis of flowers. It was so simple, it entailed little sacrifice. I could pay some contemplated visits, and leave them in possession.

I hurried on, I looked for those drab backs, the bouquet of faded flowers on the hat, the lemon-coloured blouse. They were nowhere to be seen. I must have dreamed over my idea too long. London had engulfed them. They would never sit in my porch and hear the birds twittering under the eaves.

II

I take credit that I have not husbanded my rustic happiness, nor been selfish. Indeed, an excess of hospitality through a lovely summer brought me to such a state of exhaustion that I fled abroad for a respite. Those fetchings and takings to the station, those trains missed by guests, those delayed meals, those intricate arrangements of time and place by letters, those hours of incessant talk, the anxious blending of temperaments, those minor importances of flowers, soap, towels and baths, to say nothing of variations of food and drink, the provision of note-paper and pens that write, of the desired newspaper, those last gifts of flowers and fruit, those Monday morning early risings and rushes to the station, those aftermaths of exhaustion and silence, and the endless irritation of despatching forgotten articles, all these were the inevitable concomitants of hospitality, in which I hope the pleasure received by me was not in excess of that given.

There was an historic Sunday when the spontaneous arrival of eighteen guests for tea suggested to an actress friend the loan of a board 'House Full.' Happily, occasions like these are as rare as the weather that provokes them.

One year in Venice I was excited by the discovery of a bookbinder who told me he was a direct descendant of a family that had bound books for the Aldine Press.

True or not, I cannot imagine that his ancestors showed more skill in their craft. In the dark shop almost within shadow of the ancient convent of Santa Zaccaria, where Bellini's Santa Cecilia plays her unheard music before the smiling Madonna, I found a great store of tempting objects. There were racks of handmade Venetian paper, stamped with lions, crocodiles, and fleurs-de-lys, in blue, red and green. There were boxes, pen trays, waste-paper baskets, blotters, all lined with these jolly papers. But these things were only a side-line. At the back of the shop long-haired Venetians, with eyes and faces like pages in a Carpaccio, bent over stitching machines. Girls, with pale brows and red mouths that would have delayed Casanova come to collect a folio on necromancy, deftly trimmed book edges and tooled backs.

I found a dozen reasons for dallying in that dark exciting shop. I selected backs and coverings from old vellums rolled out for my inspection. I had my manuscripts and proof-sheets bound in half vellum with Venetian endpapers. And when I had exhausted this excitement, despairing of another excuse for visiting a place where I rubbed shoulders with the Secret Ten, the Procurators of San Marco, masked gallants and dominoed revellers fresh from listening to a *toccata* of Galuppi's in a palazzo on the Grand Canal, I suddenly found a delightful volume, with blank pages and deckled edges, and bought it.

My old bookbinder asked me what I would like on the title label. In a moment of soaring ambition, perhaps unbalanced by the atmosphere of the place,

I rashly said, "Put 'Poems by Cecil Roberts.'" That I was unbalanced the subsequent five years bore proof. For ten long years I had been barren of song. The fervid years of a youth deluged in verse, in a spate of sonnets, quatrains, lyrics, elegies, long narrative poems, and poetic dramas, had ended in an unbroken drought. Why, in that shop, I should suddenly believe the font would flow again, covering two hundred pages of blank Venetian paper, I do not know.

I bought the book thus vainly labelled, and for five years it stood mockingly on my bookshelves. Then a day came, in Pilgrim Cottage, when I found its use. It is now my guest book, with many names enscribed of those to whom the Fountain Arethusa has proved more lavish. It was not this Venetian book but a summer's day beneath my apple tree that finally broke a silence of fifteen years, and set the numbers flowing again.

Like most guest books it is too often remembered when the guests have just gone, else might its two hundred names be trebled. Someone, inspecting its entries, dubbed it the Tauchnitz Catalogue of British and American Authors. But my most cherished visitors are not named in it, the birds whose antics rob me of hours of industry and, poor ornithologist that I am, whose names I do not often know. I am learning, and as I learn I am more and more mystified by these inhabitants under my roof, in my trees, hedges, and odd corners of my garden. To them belongs this place more than to me. I am becoming aware that I can only be regarded as a transitory intruder, that for years they have known aspects of my roof, my chimney-

pots, my shed, trees, lawn and garden which I can
never know. It is really I who am allowed here, to
sleep, dig and potter around, observed first with re-
sentment and suspicion, and treated now with watchful
tolerance.

There are some mysteries I would like solved concerning the birds that live around me. The more I
observe them the more I am puzzled by their instinct
or intelligence. Seeing my delight in these birds, my
secretary thoughtfully built a bird-tray and put it on
a perch in front of the window where I am supposed to
work. Actually most of my writing is done lying on
a couch, with the lid of a Tate sugar-box on my knees
for a desk. But I have an official desk which serves
for more general work, and the top of this just reaches
to the window, where I looked out across the lawn on
to a trellis of ramblers.

For a day or so nothing came to the bird-table by
the window, and then it suddenly became popular.
There was a host of gobbling hedge-sparrows. One
mother brought her brood of five. All the children
fluffed out their feathers and opened their enormous
mouths, setting up a fearful clamour. The mother
proceeded to put food into their beaks, but the astonishing thing about this feat was its regularity. She never
fed them out of turn. One-two-three-four-five, she
went, running along before them as they sat on the
ledge.

At least twice a day for a fortnight she brought her
family, always after the vulgar horde had gone, and
never once did she break the progressive order of
feeding. One-two-three-four-five, and a rap on the

head for any little beggar that fell out of line. I would like to have proved that they sat in the same order for each meal, but this was beyond detection. What I want to know is, did Mrs. Sparrow deliberately preserve that order to ensure fair play in feeding? A friend of mine, a bird lover with an amazing knowledge and eye for birds, assures me it was mere chance. But never once on all those occasions did the mathematical order fail.

Among the visitors to the bird-table, aloof and determined to dine alone, were a pair of starlings. They were vaguely familiar to me. Somewhere we had met before. Sleek, slim and well-groomed, their manners were so impeccable at my table that, if birds wore public school ties, I should have looked expecting to find they were Wykehamists. Louis was certain they were Etonians, in their black tails. But it was not at Eton or Winchester we had met. Then one day the problem was solved.

There is an exciting grocer's shop in Piccadilly. All grocers' shops are exciting to me, with their variety of odours, their barrels of butter, boxes of fruit, canisters of coffee, and gossip with young assistants in white jackets, and a pale young woman in a cash tower who gives you fourpence change without taking her eye off the place where the heroine has just decided to get into the strange young man's taxi. There is always a sad ham being sliced to death with a knife like a sultan's scimitar, and a glass case with a blue bottle preserved among the crystallised fruits.

But the grocer's shop in Piccadilly has excitements beyond most grocers' shops. There are quails in

aspic and jars of honey from Mount Hybla; to quote
Flecker, they

> . . . *have rose-candy, they have spikenard,*
> *Mastic and cerebinth and oil and spice,*
> *And such sweet jams meticulously jarred*
> *As God's own Prophet eats in Paradise.*

On many a grey morning I have turned in at the
doors of this delectable bazaar, to which the tropic
earth, the Antarctic sea and the Mediterranean shore
have made their contributions of taste and colour. The
grocery was presided over by two sleek young men,
with patent-leather shoes and patent-leather hair; the
crease in their flawless trousers suggested that they
wore another pair to sit down in. Their black tail-coats
upheld the honour of Savile Row. They were attentive but never pressing. They used their order pads
as the Edwardian beau used the dance cards of débu-
tantes. Their manners were so perfect, they blended
deference with reserve so admirably that you were not
sure whether they were peers' sons become grocers, or
grocers destined to bcome peers.

Then, one morning, watching the pair of starlings,
I recognised them. They were my grocers, Messrs.
Fortnum and Mason! For three months they were
with us, and then they disappeared. Seeking con-
solation from their prototypes, faintly believing in the
transmigration of souls, I went to the Piccadilly shop.
The twin starlings of the grocery floor had flown also!

There was something mysterious in that dual disappearance. It was in October, the month of migra-

tion. Had they, like my starlings, gone south? Might they be found in a sunny *épicerie*, or *pasticceria*? As for Messrs. Fortnum and Mason, doubtless they sat chirping on some Algerian kasbah, perhaps observing their Piccadilly friends.

Then, again, I am puzzled by the habits of a certain piebald wagtail. He is a handsome little fellow, with a black skull-cap and an oscillating tail. His black and white garb exactly matches the black timber and white walls of my cottage. He has a favourite observation post, on the ridge of the roof just by the chimney-stack. I also have a favourite position. My garden chair is placed under an apple tree for shade, where I can see the angle of the house, the garden gate, a stretch of lawn, and at evening, the sunset reddening the beechwoods on the hillside.

We are quite aware of one another from our respective positions. He watches me writing, and I watch him worming. He has a favourite small patch of lawn over which he ceaselessly runs, a little handicapped I am certain by the uncontrollable oscillation of his tail. I recommend this oscillation to the attention of the Weights and Measures Department of the Board of Trade. They are ever seeking a just balance for the nation's shopkeepers. The anatomy of that tail might reveal a more perfect fulcrum than the agate bed of the shopkeepers' scales.

But the problem I propose does not concern the *modus operandi* of the tail. My wagtail, surely the same one, appears always in the first week of August, and sits on the roof for some seven days. He never comes before, and he always comes alone. I assume he enjoys some form of domestic bliss earlier in the year. Has he deserted his wife and family, or is he a grass widower? He seems perfectly content with a celibate life. He sits alone, and walks alone. But why is he only visible the first week in August, and what brings him each year? Surely he is the same bird?

The speckled thrush is a firm friend, but I do not like the way he pushes other birds off the tray. Even the obstreperous sparrow gives him a wide berth. Yet I like his robust appearance, as well as his exquisite fluting at evening on the top bough of my apple tree, and never is his voice so lovely as when he sings after rain. Can he really hear a worm turn? Certainly the manner in which he cocks his head aside and watches the earth with a sharp eye bears out this testimony to his hearing.

I doubt whether he is very intelligent. All the other birds knew exactly when I came forth with food for the tray. They would sit around on the eaves and scold me when I was late, but the thrushes were often so long discovering food had arrived that the sparrows had gobbled up most of it when they made an appearance. Then, too, the young thrushes were recklessly careless, and their parents did little to warn them of danger. In an evil moment someone presented me with a cat, saying that an old house without a cat looked strange, and that without one I should be overrun with mice. Thus trouble began.

I do not propose to embark on a cat and dog controversy. You might as well umpire a debate between a glib young Pacifist and a morose old General. The two schools are irreconcilable. Frankly, I dislike cats as much as I can dislike anything. Most of them are nothing but a creeping lust for meat. Every cat is a sadist and prolongs the infliction of pain to the uttermost limit. But I cannot be unkind to anything, and Jimmy was tolerated in the face of monstrous crimes. He had a complete contempt for me and my household. From a kitten up he would never allow himself to be petted. He was a sly thief, a night-prowler, a miserable whiner at all times. After three years of absolute deception 'he' produced a litter of six kittens, without even betraying that he was 'in an interesting condition,' as prudish gossips say. I am still convinced that Jimmy was a hermaphrodite. Even a vet shook his head at him.

But unlike the laws of our unenlightened age, I regard sex misfits as clinical not criminal. I could have tolerated this whiner but for his tireless butchery of birds. He, or she, made my lawn a shambles. I found feathers under my chairs, I heard heart-rending scuf-flings and screechings in the bushes, with commotion of distressed parents in the branches.

I once caught Jimmy in the very act, and swung him deliriously by the tail until finally he dropped the bird. I have never heard language so foul as that he spat at me when I picked up his prey. It was a fat young thrush, bleeding at the breast. I carried it into the house and laid it on a cushion. The cat's teeth must have punctured a lung. The hæmorrhage made breathing difficult. I would never have believed, without hearing, the noise of that bird's stertorous breathing. It filled the room. The bird took five minutes to die. Just before the end it spread a wing in a feeble gesture to Life. Then the wing shivered and fell and the eyes glazed over. It moved me, as long ago I was moved in bloody Flanders.

In a moment of weak kindness I had allowed Jimmy to retain one kitten. I foolishly hoped that it would respond to affection, but it never responded to anything except meat and milk. It grew up more hateful and bloodthirsty than its mother. It had the additional horror of being cross-eyed. I hoped this would prevent it catching birds, but my hopes were dashed in the very first days of spring.

After a short absence I returned to find that Jimmy had disappeared. I was greatly relieved, but could not hide some anxiety over his fate. I accused my secretary of slaughter. "I assure you that cat's alive," he said. "Where?" I demanded. "Do you want to see him again?" "No," I replied hastily. "Then don't bother about him," was the answer.

Jimmy's son continued in crime. Being young, we had foolish hopes of reforming him. I bought a collar with bells, as a warning of his approach. He performed an epileptic dance and then dashed out through the hedge. He was back that evening without the collar, though it had been strapped on to a point of asphyxiation. When I narrated the mystery to a farmer's wife she showed no surprise, but said solemnly, "You don't surprise me. Cats can go into an exaltation and pass through anything!" But I firmly refused to accept any cat as an exalted animal, despite the Egyptians. It was some days before I realised the good woman meant an exhalation.

A cat without any endearing qualities is a trial of the flesh, and yet I am not ruthless enough to dispose of my slayer. When spring approaches I become apprehensive. Every screech in the garden sends me rushing out fearful that murder is being perpetrated. I would not have a single bird slain in my garden. I have always regarded people who indulge in hunting and shooting as a class to be prayed for, however charming they are individually. I come of hunting stock, but remain a renegade to tradition. I cheer the escaping fox and the unbagged bird.

I am well aware that Nature is relentless and cruel, that the fox is merciless in the farmyard, that some birds are parricides, and none has mercy for the worm. But I regard all this as some defect in Creation, and hold that, as an intelligent being, it is one's duty to minimise the cruelty of Nature, and not add to the total of its crimes. That my attitude can be proved illogical, I am aware. The fruit grower can be brought to ruin by thieving birds. But I am no fruit grower, and my garden, at least, shall be a bird sanctuary. They can take all my fruit, and I shall still feel I owe them a debt of song.

Those evenings of spring, those autumn mornings when sunshine follows early rain and the freshened grass is positively luminous, how often, through what hours of enchanted idleness I have sat listening to that orchestra of voices, each tuning and fluting, with little flights of piccolo and oboe, with experimental passages *pizzicato*, and lyric bursts from thrush and blackbird, *divas* impatient in the leafy side wings of the garden-theatre! Young Paris gave one apple to

his selected beauty.   Since selection is impossible among
so many beauties, they can have all mine.

I have a friend, a fruit grower who is also a bird
lover.   He has solved the problem ingeniously, the
more so as he has turned the cat's lust for killing to
some good purpose.   There was a year when he felt
almost driven to the gun.   His cherry trees were
stripped of unripe fruit, his logans were all consumed
by blackbirds.   The bullfinch and sparrow removed all
the buds of gooseberry and red currant during a cold
spell in March, although his bird-trays were full of
food.   He did not want to go to the expense of having
rattles going from dawn to sunset, and in any case it is
useless.

Suddenly, the run of a cat between two cherry trees
gave him an idea.   The movement of that cat kept the
birds away, but often she deserted her beat and appeared from the bushes with a bird in her mouth.   My
friend ran a wire some forty yards long under his fruit-
trees, tying each end to a trunk.   He then placed a
collar and a lead on the cat and attached the lead, with
a ring, to the wire.   The cat spent its time running
up and down its beat, and when it was tired lay on a
box under the branches.   Whenever a bird appeared
she pounced and ran along the wire.   The result was
that the presence of the cat kept the birds away.   Even
the cat seemed to enjoy the performance, for she made
no effort to break away from the lead.   Certainly my
friend's cats thrived on their policeman's pay.   I suggested hanging a few bells on the line to tell when they
were at work.

I constantly find myself puzzled by the degree of

bird intelligence. They have memories, we know, and a sense of time as well as of season. Strange to relate, they are colour-blind, although their sense of sight is highly developed beyond that of all other vertebrates. They cannot see blue or violet, only colours towards the opposite end of the spectrum. They have a marvellous system of 'central heating.' Regulation of body temperature is effected automatically by a thermostatic nerve-centre in the brain. When the blood temperature changes, this centre is stimulated by the bloodstream, sending nervous impulses to the muscles, the skin and elsewhere, and regulating the production and loss of heat.

They are strangely illogical in some respects and farsighted in others. Why, for instance, are they so afraid of me when I sit at my desk behind the closed windows? They fly off the tray the moment they see me, but if the window is open I can move as much as I like without frightening them. Does the glass make a monster of me in the bird's eye? Nearly every day in the birds' drinking bowl I will find a half-eaten worm. It cannot possibly have crawled there. It must have been dropped in by a bird. Like ill-mannered children, do birds drink with their mouths full and spill the worm?

Is it instinct or observation that warns the crow not to build in the apparently strong branch of an elm, which is actually worm-eaten and liable to break in a gale?

Several excursions in bird surgery have made me extremely doubtful of the assertion that sick birds are killed off by their fellows. I am wondering whether this birdicide is not conditional. It is wonderful what can be done for wounded birds and animals with a little patience and ingenuity.

One day in a country inn I heard some rustics telling their companions about a hen that had a wooden leg. The whole taproom roared with laughter, whereupon the man who told the story grew indignant and said he would bet anyone ten shillings there was such a hen, and he could take him to see it. I thought the chance of seeing a hen with a wooden leg was well worth ten shillings, and promptly made the bet, and offered to transport him and any who cared to go with us to the farm in question. So four of us set off to see the hen with a wooden leg.

After motoring some three miles we drew up at a farmhouse and our guide went in to find the farmer. There emerged a man who looked less like a farmer than anyone I have ever seen. He was young, pale, bespectacled, and rather shy in manner. The story, he told us, was wrong in one detail, it was a cock with a wooden leg. One morning the bird was seen trailing a leg that had been almost bitten off in some mysterious way. It was obvious that the leg would never mend, so an amputation was performed with a pair of scissors, and the stump bound up. The farmer told us that as soon as the bird was released he flew off to the farmyard, where he sat on the wall and crowed loudly, as if announcing his operation to the hens.

A few days later, when the stump was healed up, the cock was captured and measured for a wooden leg. The farmer took a small piece of oak, with a flange at one end. At the other end he cut a socket half an inch deep, making a splint. He then placed the cock's bony stump in the socket and bound it with an old violin string, much as one binds a cricket bat. He told us he had intended it for a humorous experiment. Certainly he expected the cock would soon devise a means of ridding himself of his crutch. When the cock ran off with a tremendous hullabaloo, he was staggered to see it running wildly on both legs, in its hysteria quite forgetting the wooden one.

Every day the farmer went to look at the cock, and there it was walking about, the wooden leg in full use! A week passed, and a fortnight. The cock seemed quite unaware that he possessed a false leg. At feeding time he could run with the best. Gradually the fame of the bird spread, and an enterprising vicar solicited its services for a garden fête, where it gave four profitable exhibitions, decoyed across the lawn with grain.

The farmer took us out into the field while he was narrating this history, and there, lording it over his hens, stalked the proud cock! He was captured, and we examined the wooden leg. When he was released he ran off, without even a limp. The bet was well won.

The young farmer said to me with a twinkle in his eye. "I've seen him beating his wives with his wooden leg!" When I asked what had given him the idea, he laughed. "Family tradition, I suppose. Three generations of us have run a surgical appliances business. I took to farming, because I was consumptive."

The cock with the wooden leg brings me to my own story of manipulative surgery. One day in the lane above my cottage we found a wounded goldfinch. It was easily captured, and the shoulder of the left wing proved to be broken. The accident, however it happened, must have been recent, for a raw wound was still bleeding. The problem of resetting the wing and keeping the bird quiet during the healing was difficult. Finally, we evolved an experimental method. To keep the bird from attempting to move its wing, which would have been fatal to the setting of the bones, we passed a strong rubber band over its body and wings. After a few vain efforts to flutter the goldfinch became reconciled to the band.

There remained the resetting of the wing. We next bound the wing with strong court plaster, which acted as a mould, and then placed the bird, together with water and seed, in a large box with steep sides, on the roof of the garage, away from cats and frightening noises. The goldfinch settled down at once, ate and drank, and hopped about in the box.

The following morning the bird was still alive and showed no nervousness when we came to feed him. During the day we noticed that he was visited by other goldfinches, and we had fears that, in accordance with the legend, they would attack and kill the wounded bird. But nothing of the kind happened. The visitors merely sat on the edge of the box and chattered. I am sure they uttered sympathetic and encouraging words.

After three days we took off the rubber band but left the court plaster binding on the wing shoulder. The bird at once began to flutter about, and he was obviously stiff, but the pleasing feature was that he used both wings equally as he fluttered around the box. We had a final glimpse of him that evening, sleeping in a corner. The next morning he had gone, and we had no doubt that, the numbness vanished from his wings, he had flown back to freedom.

III

There is one other bird I must mention, not a visitor, but an inhabitant of a golden cage. He is a canary with bright feathers, and by birth a Frenchman. He was brought from Paris, a present for me from my secretary. He is an excellent and reliable songster, filling the house with his morning salute. Often I take his cage up to the landing, where I hang it outside the guest's bedroom. This room has a little sliding window looking on to the landing, which I had made in order to give a current of air through the tiny room, and also to afford a vista, through the dormer window opposite, of the hillside and the beechwoods.

A guest, therefore, is often awakened by loud bird-song coming through the sliding window, and is always enthusiastic about this songster that visits my garden. Then, rising, he finds it is a tame bird in a cage, singing in full-throated ease. The song ended, a little coaxing is tried, but the guest is observed by a beady eye. Further whistling and a 'tweet-tweet' having failed to encourage the bird, something in those fixed eyes arouses suspicion, and the hoax is unmasked.

For it is a mechanical bird, with moving head, beak and tail. A key under the cage provides a series of warblings, amazingly deceptive, that can be made continuous or intermittent, according to the setting of a lever. One of my guests lost his temper somewhat when he found he had been hoaxed. He had assured the servant who brought his morning tea that he had never heard birds sing so well anywhere else! He told me I had no right to let a mechanical bird make a fool of him in front of the servant. But he was very eager the next morning that we should play the trick on a new guest who had come overnight.

I had first encountered and been enchanted by one of these mechanical birds in a friend's flat in Piccadilly. It was singing lustily in a sunny window overlooking the Green Park when the butler ushered me in. I had heard no such music in mid-winter since I had heard the canaries in the palm court of the Sevilla-Biltmore at Havana, where their shrilling in the glorious December sunshine was deafening.

The Piccadilly bird quite deceived me, until the spring ran down, and I tried to coax another song from it. For a considerable time I searched for a mechanical bird, but they are rare in England, and such specimens as I found in antique shops either croaked, sang absurdly, or had moulted obscenely. It was my secretary, Louis Tissier, who, remembering my quest, had found a shop in Paris full of these singing birds. He confided that he had brought it through the Customs as a stuffed bird. "Why stuffed?" I asked. "Well, if it sang it would have been taxed as a musical instrument!" he replied.

Sometimes I speculate on the origin of this artificial bird. It comes from Paris, certainly, but has it descended from the workshop of some ingenious German toymaker? There are suggestions that its

The Study

origin is even deeper in history. Its kind may first have
seen the light in the miraculous gardens of Baghdad
or Constantinople. It is likely the Sultan Haroun al-
Raschid had a mechanical bird in his famous garden.
There was intense rivalry between Baghdad and Constantinople, and we do know that the splendour-loving
Emperor Theophilus possessed mechanical birds. He
had, indeed, a mechanical garden. Trees of gilded
bronze lined the approach to the throne, and on their
branches, amid fruit and leaves of rubies, turquoises,
sapphires, emeralds and pearls, there perched jewelled
and golden birds that lifted their voices in praise of the
Emperor.

In one respect only my bird recalls Hans Andersen's
magic nightingale. My bird moves his tail up and
down as he sings. "As soon as the artificial bird had
been wound up," he wrote, "it could sing one of the
pieces that the real bird sang, and then it would move its
tail up and down, all glittering with silver and gold."

Unlike Hans Andersen's precocious nightingale, my
bird has no tail glittering with silver and gold. Its appearance is anything but gorgeous, and one unkind
friend said it had the face of a Parish Worker. But I
hope that, unlike the royal nightingale, promoted to sit
on a silk cushion and be the Grand Imperial Toilet-
Table Singer, something inside my bird will not 'snap
with a bang.'

IV

The end of September is a depressing time for the
bird lover. Only the robins contrive to be cheerful
amid all the commotion in the bird world. I remember

watching, in the steady downpour of a September day, when the first fire had to be lit in the study, and outside everything dripped, a fat robin who discovered a puddle in my garden path. How delighted the little urchin was! He squatted in it, ducking himself, head and body, and, catching my eye, he repeated the performance to show me how good it was. But I did not feel so cheerful, for an evil augury had been fulfilled.

That morning, while shaving at my bedroom window, which looks on to the wooded hillside, I had observed a crowd of house martins sitting along the telegraph wires. It was like nine o'clock at a cinema, there was not a seat left. For days they had been gathering, and the thought of their migration south, and the winter coming, saddened me. Like a Roman augur I saw in those birds an omen. I was right.

Downstairs, an excellent housekeeper who had made my house spotless and my summer without care, told me she was going. When I recovered from the shock she said she was afraid of being alone in the country in winter, and had taken a place in town. She was sorry to go, but she dare not stay. Like the house martins the housekeeper did not relish the long dark winter.

I knew it was useless to persuade her to stay, and my argument could not have been very sound, since I was moving to town myself, and the New Year would probably find me on the Riviera. If only she had been like that robin, robustly cheerful in the rain and the puddles!

The puddle-bath performance, therefore, did not arouse my enthusiasm, and I watched the robin gloomy-eyed. The lawn was untidy with yellow leaves, the plants in the garden were cut down, my noble chestnut tree would soon be stripped by the first frost. One morning, when I looked out of my window, the telegraph wires would be as bare as the trees; there would not be a single martin wanting a seat.

Well, it is pleasant to think the emigrants remain British. I am told they follow a familiar route along the Atlantic seaboard, cross to the African continent where the seas narrow, and land eventually on the Indian Ocean side of South Africa. So having left our shores they form a British colony on the other side of the world.

WINTERING SOUTH

Winter approaches, the Martins are going South.
  Strange! Though they know quite well where
    they're going to stay,
They can't give me any addresses by word of mouth,
  Nor leave them in writing, nor cable them on their way.

Young Martin remembers a bungalow built on the shore,
  Where the long white rollers break on the African sand:
Old Martin goes back to the villa he had before,
  Where a homesick planter dreams of his native land.

And Blackcap, who raided my orchard and twittered
    at me,
  Finds the nights very cold though the tropical days
    are hot,
So houses himself in a thick-leaved banana tree,
  And fattens himself, sings little and dozes a lot.

Wise birds!   When I want to go South I have much to do,
  Tickets to get and a passport and suitable clothes,
A seat reserved at Victoria or Waterloo,
  The Channel to cross, or a sea that a landsman loathes.

So I watch you with envy, old friends who made summer
    so gay,
  Lined up on the telegraph wires preparing for flight.
Bon Voyage!   The leaves in my garden are falling, the
    day
  Grows shorter.   Wise birds, who warned you of frost
    in the night?

CHAPTER VII

TULIPPOMANIA

AND now let us go back to the garden which I have shamefully neglected. Some of us are born gardeners, some of us have gardening thrust upon us. Tilly, whom we left in the garden, was shocked by the condition of my crimson rambler. It was due, not only to the montbretia she found choking the roots, but also to the need of drastic thinning.

"That's dead, and that—and that!" she exclaimed mercilessly, walking along. "You see, it's all shot up along the top of the trellising. You must cut out this —to give the young runners a chance."

The secateurs were in her hand. She gave a vicious cut to a sturdy brier, and laughed at my dismay.

"It's no use, you simply must be drastic. Now you'll have to get all that out," she said. "You'll tear your skin and swear horribly, so do it after I've gone. Take a tip, when you're cutting ramblers, cut them out in two-foot lengths. If you don't they'll get you like a constrictor."

Alas, the next day I ignored her warning! With pride I pulled out a length of dead rambler, when suddenly it came for me like a rattlesnake. There was an ugly scratch down my face and neck, and in the attempt to ward off the thing I lacerated my hand. I treat old ramblers now like small boys treat worms.

Tilly's revelation of my abysmal ignorance sent me

hastily to gardening books. I closed most of them in utter despair.

The work one had to do to rear a simple flower! "You've been reading gardening books," said a clever neighbour, when I babbled of mulches and composts. "Take no notice of 'em, and go up the beech avenue with a bucket. That thick black loam you find there's worth all your composts."

Later, I was agitated by a gentleman who lives in Holland. In some mysterious way he found out that I lived in a cottage. He addressed me very cordially as "My very good Sir (or Madam)." There was something very charming and touching about his letter. "I sincerely hope you will not refrain from entrusting your order to your dear old bulb-grower." At once I felt an impulse to write to my dear old bulb-grower. It was all so friendly.

And then he destroyed my night's rest, the wretch. I opened his letter late in the evening, for I had scornfully regarded the envelope as the bearer of a sale catalogue. The covering letter read, with its friendly air, I turned to the bulb catalogue.

Much have I travell'd in the realms of gold,
And many goodly states and kingdoms seen;

thus Keats on first looking into Chapman's *Homer*. Stout Cortez was not more silent with wonder than I, on first looking into Herr Telgom's bulb catalogue. I finished it in a state of intoxication. I saw my garden blooming as never garden bloomed. What's in a name?—often far more than there is in the bulb of that name. I am not sure now whether I did not derive more intense pleasure from the names of these bulbs, with such prodigious promise of colour and shape, than ever I derived from the bulbs themselves, even though they justified my old bulb-grower's prophecies. Dead must he be of soul who is not stirred by the offer of *Incomparabilis* Sir Watkin (perianth, sulphur; cup, bright yellow). I ordered a dozen Sir Watkins, for seven and threepence, and a dozen *Incomparabilis* Macebearers, that he might come with real pomp.

Daffodils of any variety are dear to me. Shakespeare loved them, and Wordsworth. I remember as a small boy walking miles, with aching feet, to Gowborrow Park, where Wordsworth had seen them:

> *. . . a crowd,*
> *A host, of golden daffodils;*
> *Beside the lake, beneath the trees,*
> *Fluttering and dancing in the breeze.*

So I ordered a host, trumpets, cupped and double. Then I turned to the tulips. Their names read like an enchantment. "These Darwins," wrote Herr Telgom, with something of a poet's ecstasy, "are the most lovely flowers among Tulips we know, so stately, so graceful and bright and cheery." Even had they been solemn I could not have resisted such distinguished guests in my beds as the Baronne de La Tonnaye (rose), Madame Krelage (rosy-pink), Victoire d'Oliviera (dark red) among the ladies, and among the gentlemen Philip de Comines (although mahogany), Professor Rauwenhof (suspiciously cherry-red), the Sultan (maroon black), Rev. H. Ewbank (silvery heliotrope), and William Pitt and Whistler. I added Mr. Farncombe Sanders, of whom I knew nothing, except that he was rose-scarlet, and, I was certain, of some importance.

I confess now that I was carried away by my dear old bulb-grower. He had many jolly little bulbs as well as pompous ones. When he offered me a rainbow mixture of cottage tulips, 'beloved in England,' I could not resist. It was enticing to be able to buy a dozen Mrs. Asquiths for one and threepence, and keep them under severe restraint in an obscure corner. Mrs. Asquith was a narcissus. I looked down the list in vain for a bulbous Lloyd George, it being my mischievous intention to put them in a bed together and let them fight it out.

When my list was completed I was a little dismayed to discover I had ordered five hundred bulbs. I reflected that I need not plant them all, and it was better to have too many rather than too few. The letter posted, I waited for days in a state of suppressed anxiety. Then one morning a railway company's dray drew up at my garden door. A man deposited a large crate. The bulbs had come. It seemed to me that the garden had burst into flower at once.

Let it be said I was not the first to lose my head over tulips. It seems there is a well-known disease called Tulippomania. It was brought from Holland to England by William III. The Dutch Government had been compelled to take drastic steps against the tulip enthusiasts, and they finally had to impose a limit on the price of a single bulb. A Semper Augustus had risen, during the fever, to fourteen thousand florins, and then collapsed to fifty. Men were ruined by tulips. The craze invaded England. Addison had a strange adventure among the tulip lunatics. He had taken refuge in a storm and overheard a most extraordinary conversation.

"I was surprised to hear one say that he valued the Black Prince more than the Duke de Vendosme. How the Black Prince should become a rival of the Duke de Vendosme I could not conceive; and was more startled when I heard a second affirm, with great vehemence, that if the Emperor of Germany was not going off, he should like him better than either of them. He added that, though the season was changeable, the Duke of Marlborough was in blooming beauty. I was wondering to myself from whence they had received this odd intelligence; especially when I heard them mention the names of several other generals, as the Prince of Hesse and King of Sweden, who, they said, were both running away. To which they added, what I entirely agreed with them in, that the Crown of France was very weak, but that the Marshal Villars still kept his colours. At last, one of them told the company, if they would go along with him, he would show them a Chimney-sweeper and a Painted Lady in the same bed, which he was sure would please them very much."

This was too much for Addison. He made his presence known and was invited along with the party. One of his hosts seemed a plain honest man "had not his head been touched with that distemper which Hippocrates calls the Tulippomania, inasmuch that he would talk very rationally on any subject in the world but a tulip. He told me that he valued the bed of flowers which lay before us, and was not above twenty yards in length and two in breadth, more than he would the best hundred acres of land in England."

No one can say that a bulb is a romantic object. Neither its name nor its appearance inspires thoughts of beauty. When the bulbs were all unpacked, and lay on the garage floor, grubby, oniony-looking things, I began to feel that Herr Telgom had double-Dutched me. Mrs. Asquith was insignificant, with a suspicion of a beard. *Incomparabilis* Sir Watkin was a poor-looking object, and the incomparable Macebearers were contemptible.

My heart sank as I examined these dismal bulbs. Fool that I was to be deceived by the eloquence of that ecstatic Dutchman! It seemed to me in that disillusioned mood that there was far more promise in the string of onions hanging in the corner of the garage. Whatever those onions might or might not become, they were most cunningly woven in a string and brought back a pleasant memory.

One morning my garden gate had been opened and a sturdy youth of about seventeen came down the garden path carrying a frightful burden of onions slung over his shoulder. I saw at a glance that he was one of those bands of Breton peasants who invade this country at the close of the onion season. I had often seen them working in pairs in London and wondered at their enterprise in entering a vast foreign city, with no knowledge of English, and only a few strings of onions between them and destitution. They were, to me, always a singular sight in London, but I had never expected to see them in the heart of the country.

The Breton youth with the onions stood for a moment surveying the unfamiliar scene, and then discovered the kitchen-window, where he attracted the attention of my housekeeper. A tremendous battle of wills was quickly in progress. My housekeeper was quite determined not to buy onions. The Breton was determined she should. The argument was none the less fierce because neither disputant understood one word the other said. But the face of the youth was marvellously eloquent. He was deeply hurt at the contempt with which his excellent onions were treated. He thrust a string of them under the housekeeper's nose, loudly protesting in his Breton patois.

His hands were eloquent too. They were fine, expressive hands, surprising in a peasant. The price, according to his fingers, had already fallen from three shillings a string to two. His dark, handsome face now assumed such a pathetic expression that I wondered how my housekeeper had the heart to refuse the offer. But refuse she did, and when at last he came down to one and six and she remained adamant, I intervened.

He greeted me with the neatest of bows, and when I addressed him in French his face lit up. But his own patois was beyond comprehension. After some questioning I learned that with a companion he was travelling, with Reading as a centre. It was his first visit to England. He was seventeen.

I tried to find out the finances of this onion-selling.

It seemed they were sent over from St. Malo by a man who organised the canvassing. They were given areas to work, an allowance of a shilling a day and commission. On a good day they made four shillings in commission, never more, for their sales were limited by the weight of the onions they could carry. A consignment had been sent to Reading, where they could renew their supplies.

I asked to feel the weight of the onions he was carrying. It was as much as I could lift. The youth pulled back his shirt from his shoulder and showed me a red weal where the cords pressed. Where had he come from? St. Pol-de-Léon, near Cap Finistère. Would he be glad to get back? Oh no, there was nothing at home. He lived with an old mother. His father was dead, a fisherman, drowned. Two brothers were dead, fishermen, drowned. Would he be a fisherman? He shrugged his shoulders and smiled. Perhaps, after he had done his Service. But his mother was against it. There were three girls; he was the only boy.

It was lunch-time. I told my housekeeper to give him a meal in the kitchen. They smiled, full of respect for each other after their battle. It was during lunch that some memory haunting me was defined. I jumped up and went to my bookshelves. Of course! St. Pol-de-Léon was the birthplace of Mon frère Yves, Loti's Breton sailor, who had grown up under a cloud because the Curé had forbidden the ringing of bells at his baptism. "Ces Kermadec sont des gens qui jamais ne donnent rien à l'offrande, et le père dépense au cabaret tout son avoir."

These onions brought by the Breton lad looked far more promising than Herr Telgom's bulbs. I felt tempted to pull some off the string and plant them. As I stood ruefully looking at my purchase, spread across the garage floor, my gardener came in. I invited his opinion.

"Where are you goin' to plant 'em, sir? There ain't no room in the garden."

"But surely we can make a display?" I said.

"Well——"

Silence.

"They'll come up, I suppose?" I enquired.

"They may and they mayn't."

This is the stock reply.

"But they're Dutch bulbs," I emphasised. I checked myself from adding "From my dear old bulb-grower."

"They're no better for that, sir."

I felt snubbed. It was the time of the 'Buy British' campaign in the newspapers, following a campaign urging us not to buy anything in a time of national crisis.

The gardener left me. I stared at the multitude of bulbs, for which I now had no enthusiasm. Over-whelmed, I went indoors. Later in the afternoon I recovered courage. Those bulbs had to be planted, or I could not put the car back into the garage.

I went upstairs and got into my garden uniform. This consists of a two-piece suit that I bought for five shillings at a sports outfitters in the Hohestrasse in Cologne. What I shall do when it is worn out I cannot think. It is made of thick blue stockinet,

with a woolly inside. The top piece is a blouse with
roll collar, a zip neck-fastener, and two sleeves with
elastics closing the cuffs over the wrists. The trousers
have an elastic band at the waist, and at each ankle.
Both articles are large enough to pull over one's clothes.
Actually it is an athlete's pullover, to keep him warm
while waiting in scanty garb for his event. Never was
five shillings better spent.

Thus clad, with heavy crêpe rubber shoes on my
feet, I went out into the garden to plant bulbs. I
planted until it was dusk, my back ached. I planted
bulbs in the beds, along the paths, under the windows,
round the tree trunks, along the edge of the lawn.
Wherever I could find a space I buried a bulb. Only in
two places was I geometric, in the beds on each side
of the path to the door. Here the sultan, the professor,
the clergyman, the statesman and the artist were carefully spaced with those rose, rosy-pink and dark-red
ladies whom Herr Telgom assured me were "so stately,
so graceful and bright and cheery."

When I had finished it was quite dark, and I could
barely see what I was doing with Mrs. Asquith round
by the Dutch oven, which protrudes from the back of
my house on to the lawn, and on which dwarf cypresses
grow. Not one of the five hundred bulbs lacked a bed
that night.

This was in October, before I went away. Through
the winter I forgot all about the bulbs. Then, with the
coming of spring, the excitement began. Spring in
any case is an exciting season. Every morning something suddenly raises its head and salutes the sun. The
iron hedge has a red tinge and the next morning a wall

of green leaf glistens with the dew. One grey morning, stooping to stroke the cat, which had appeared through his favourite hole in the privet, I saw something that made my heart stand still. A pellet of earth had been pushed on one side. I removed it. A point like a little green pencil was there. Outside in the road my car purred, waiting to take me to London. Two of my week-end guests were already in it.

Forgetting them, I examined both beds. Nothing. Then I went round the garden, anywhere that I could recall having planted bulbs. Nothing. Had my old bulb-grower failed me? No, here was the first of the five hundred. I bent down on my knees and examined that pencil point, thrust a finger tenderly round its stem. There was no doubt about it. Was it the Baronne de La Tonnaye, the Rev. Ewbank or William Pitt who had arrived? One did not know. In my excitement I could have sat down and encouraged that bulb to grow. But I went into the house before joining my wondering guests, and left strict word that a sharp look-out was to be kept and further arrivals to be reported to me in London. Then I tore myself away.

Two days later, in the morning, as I worked with my typist, the telephone rang. My housekeeper reported that over fifty tulips had arrived from their winter journey through the soil.

"There are over fifty!" I said, jubilantly, to my typist, as I replaced the receiver, and seeing her blank expression, added—"There are over fifty tulips come up in my garden this morning!"

"Oh, how wonderful!" she exclaimed.

Yes, it was wonderful, but I felt sad at the thought that I should not see them until Friday. Perhaps then there would be a hundred, perhaps two hundred. I began to feel that my dear old bulb-grower was a man of honour, despite my gardener's doubts.

In April his promises were so magnificently fulfilled that I had only one regret. I wished I had planted them all on one side of the house. For I had to walk round and round, now certain this, now certain that, was the most glorious prospect.

LINES IN HONOUR OF HERR TELGOM

Sing a song of Telgom and let the truth be said,
Four and twenty tulips all planted in a bed—
La Baronne de La Tonnaye, the Sultan, William Pitt,
The Reverend H. Ewbank and Whistler filling it.

Four and twenty bulbs set all neatly in a row,
Hidden in the dark earth, persistently they grow.
Ring the bells of Heaven, the Spring is coming fast,
All the bulbs are jumping up, none wishing to be last.

Sing a song of Telgom, my dear old bulb-grower,
Who said he was a Dutchman?—more elbow to his
power!
Not a bulb but blossoms, yellow, blue and red,
Oh, isn't it a dainty sight to see them all in bed!

CHAPTER VIII

A MONARCH COMES TO STAY

I HAVE made no pretence in these pages to be an intelligent gardener. My ignorance of things that grow and give me pleasure or displeasure results in a state of complete humility before any garden or Nature-wise person. There is my friend Francis Jekyll, for instance. He has in his veins the blue blood of gardening stock. When you read in the catalogues of nurserymen the name, 'Munstead Variety,' it denotes an eminent variety of seed or plant. Munstead was the name of Gertrude Jekyll's famous garden. She was remarkable at all times of her life. She could carve, paint and design. Her knowledge of gardening was encyclopædic, down to the smallest details, as for instance the making of pot-pourri. Some of her pot-pourri is still fragrant in my study after five years. Although she enjoyed world-wide fame as a gardener she did not take to gardening seriously until she was forty. That fills one with hope.

Her character, which was forcible even at eighty-five years of age, was expressed in numerous ways, and upon other men and women of genius. William Nicholson painted a masterpiece called 'Miss Jekyll's Boots.' It is simply a study of a pair of crinkled old garden boots, bulging and unlaced, on a table; the kind of boots you can see just put off in the entrance porch of any vicarage or country house.

My friend not only inherited the famous garden, but also his aunt's garden-genius. You can imagine the trepidation with which I watched him saunter in mine. I know few men with more surprising facets of knowledge. His interests embrace alpine flora, the works of Boehm, Bach and Goya, among other things. I was not surprised, therefore, when, descending upon me in an obscure village of the Dolomites, he proceeded in daily walks to give all that grew and bloomed around us 'a local habitation and a name.' In Venice one summer he had shown me a garden, superb beyond imagining, that flourished in a city where gardens are always surprising and often exquisite, hidden away in the folds of Settecento palaces, behind walls washed by the green water of some *rio*.

The Jekyll genius flourished in Venice, for here another aunt, Mrs. Eden, had converted a portion of an island in the lagoon, into a pleasance that was appropriately dubbed 'The Garden of Eden.' When, therefore, Francis first walked into my garden and expressed approval of its general design, I was a proud man. The design was not mine, but possession of a garden, even made by others, is nine points of the pride one feels. But as he quested about, with a suggestion of thinning there, of plants for this north patch, of shrubs for that corner, creepers for the wall, I could have burst into tears, realising then how badly this child of my heart was dressed.

It seemed to me, in that hour of revelation, that the whole garden would have to be dug up and replanted. I suggested something in this fashion, and was gently reproved. "No—no, don't punish a garden, teach it how to grow gently. Now, in that south corner put a japonica; it'll be quite happy."

I felt like a medical student following a specialist visiting the beds, with operations suggested or deferred, prescriptions given or treatment defined. I swear that sick plants lifted their heads at his touch. Am I too fanciful in thinking that, just as dogs know human lovers of their kind, so do plants? My friend could, of course, be the severe surgeon. After he had operated on a rose tree, I learned the wisdom of the saying (or something like it) 'spare the knife and spoil the bud.' I learned that few gardeners can be trusted to prune their own trees, so tender-hearted are they.

I can never quite believe experienced gardeners who assure me that it pays to pick blooms, that plants flourish when they lose their foremost blossoms. I never cut without misgiving the rose on the verge of blooming, despite the many buds that crowd the tree. Does a mother more readily produce her children because the earliest and brightest are plucked by Providence? I remember being reduced to tears in my childhood by a visiting spinster who used to sing at the piano a fearful piece called *The Heavenly Gardener*. Towards the end of the saccharine verses the awful tragedy was wailed out, *molto simpatico*—

> *Then came the Heavenly Gardener*
> *And took my Bud away.*

In the song the mother seemed to have no further buds. A study of mediæval tombs, with their rows of thirteen or fourteen children kneeling behind the parents, one half in swaddling clothes denoting death in infancy, shows that, in the good old puerperal days, drastic cropping did not discourage the parental tree.

I often wonder whether the people who motor down from town for the day, and on leaving are asked "Would you like a few flowers?" ever realise the desperate unselfishness of their hosts. It is not meanness that gives the gardener a pang when he cuts his flowers. He knows, indeed, that his plants are the better for cutting, but in his heart he wonders if the flower that goes will ever be equalled by the flower that comes. Often I have hesitated before a lovely bloom, uncertain whether to let it end its days in the garden or in the vase. The decision grows more difficult as the summer wanes and one's choice of flowers diminishes. I felt no hesitation about cutting my bunches of grapes, as grapes are obviously grown for eating. With flowers I do not feel the same. They are lovely in one's rooms, but it is just as unnatural for them to be there as fish in an aquarium.

Sometimes my conscience is soothed by the thought that cutting prolongs their lives a little, if they are properly treated in captivity. It is not sufficient merely to cut flowers and stick them in a vase. Like domestic animals they respond to kindness. I once experimented with two vases of narcissi. They were cut from the same bed at the same time. One bunch was cut and placed direct in a vase of ordinary water (Exhibit A); the other bunch was placed in a vase of rain-water, and their stalks were slit up for two inches (Exhibit B). A was left in the room all night. B was taken out of the vase and floated in water each night.

A stood in a window without sunshine, B with. The water was changed daily. I repeated the experiment twice with the same result. A lasted four days, B seven.

Most flowers respond to floating in water, but the period should be varied according to the flower; lilies of the valley, for instance, lose their scent and delicate form, and the petals become transparent if immersed too long. Red roses can be left overnight in deep water. All woody stems should be slit up and slightly forced open. Some flowers grow more lovely through their stages of decay. The large magnolia has a strangely beautiful pistil as the petals fall away, but many cannot endure magnolias in the house owing to their pungent lemon odour.

Some people are strangely susceptible to the scent of flowers and the smell of fruit. I remember the severe lecture I received from a meticulous friend who assured me it was a very wrong thing to have apples standing on my sideboard. They should be taken away into the larder. I had them removed to satisfy him, but he still complained. "You see, those apples have impregnated the whole house," he said. But when he went upstairs I think he realised any protest was use-less. The floor of the landing and all the shelves were covered with apples! The crop had been abnormal that year. I had given away large quantities, but there were still too many for my small storage place, with the result that apples filled every inch of the floors upstairs, even under the chairs on the landing.

It happened that I like the odour of stored apples, but realising that some of my guests might not, I filled the car one day and delivered the load to the matron of a hostel in which I am interested. All natural boys have a love of apple pie.

When the time came for a general replanning of my flower-beds I told my gardener that, in my eyes, a cottage garden would be perfect with seven things. He could make a show of wallflowers, snapdragons, phlox, sweet-william, delphiniums, lupins and rose trees, and I should have no complaint.

There is a little garden in front of the local post-office that fills me with envy whenever I go to post a letter. It is a village post-office, with irritating 'hours' that never coincide with one's needs. It is only a cottage, and one must ring a bell to gain admittance. Fortunately, the post-mistress, who lives all alone, never minds being disturbed. But I am baffled by her. Never can I catch her working in her garden. I once went there in full moonlight to post a letter that would not be collected until full daylight, simply for the purpose of satisfying a suspicion that she gardened by night and postmarked by day. But all I saw, in an upper window, was a shadow that told me she retired early.

Some days later, dining with the Postmaster-General, I told him about this lovely and baffling garden. I suggested that he should offer a prize for the best-kept country post-office garden. Railway companies give prizes for the best railway-station gardens, why not prizes for post-office gardens? If we did not live in an age of Budget deficits, and a gross Revenue ever panting after a grosser Expenditure, I should suggest a Floral Commissioner for the Office of Works, whose pleasant duty it would be to brighten public life, and public works, with flowers and shrubs. It is done so well in our parks that it might be equally well done in our post-offices. How nice to look at the times of delivery and collection in windows whose ledges carry boxes of lobelias, petunias and geraniums! Why not associate pillar-boxes and flower-boxes?

It is not at all a fantastic idea. I recall delightful post-offices in Tyrol villages where business is transacted under balconies ablaze with geraniums. The London house of the British Broadcasting Company has two terraces of flowers to break a precipice of stone. But I regret to say that inside I discovered a monstrous aspidistra set in a special niche, and flood-lighted! In the silent chamber, where one speaks to the listening world, the cabinet-maker and the interior decorator have done everything possible to create a scene of modern comfort, but a vase of flowers would do more than an acre of veneer to break the strain of talking to oneself in a universe of eavesdroppers.

Should the Floral Commissioner ever be appointed I shall bombard him with many suggestions. He might plant creepers to grow over some of the public statues that afflict our eyes. The atrocious memorial to Nurse Cavell might be made more symbolic of the atrocity it commemorates, if overgrown with forget-me-nots, and clad in Virginia creeper, which would redden in the very month when her blood stained the name of Germany. Some of our factory chimneys in crowded housing areas always fill me with a desire to experiment with the climbing power of a good creeper. I once inhabited a room that looked on to the chimney-stack of the Army Clothing Factory on the Thames Embankment. The architect had attempted some decoration at the top. Why are gardeners never invited to begin at the bottom? Life has produced few things more hideous than a gasometer. Are there any plants that could survive their smell and decorate their rims?

It is pleasant to observe that the modern petrol station often exhibits a floral approach. There is a rose pergola on the Bath Road that makes me aware that my tank will take more petrol. It is wonderful what enthusiasm can achieve. My Californian poppies very much excited a young French guest, Count Dedons de Pierrefeu. He put some of the seeds into his waistcoat pocket and vowed he would grow them on the window-sills of his father's apartment in the Faubourg St. Honoré. The next summer he astonished Paris, and me, with a flower-show such as the Faubourg had never seen before.

Among rapid normal growers, to cover an ugly corner, I commend the giant nasturtium. Most gardeners seem to treat the nasturtium, giant and dwarf, as beneath contempt. Its readiness to grow in the most poverty-stricken corner causes it to be scorned, like rhubarb, a fruit reared on rubbish and damned with custard on the servant's evening out.

The giant nasturtium is a gallant fellow. He will take any fence, go over the rough, and deserves a Whyte Melville among gardeners to honour his breed. What is the extent to which a giant nasturtium will send out a runner? I measured one shoot, flowering nobly in mid-October, that was seventeen feet long.

The flower was a scarlet that would have shamed a Grenadier Guard. But there is a nasturtium exciting beyond all others, of a semi-climbing variety. It comes from California, and is called the Bodgeri Golden Gleam. It is scented, and is of a deep orange-gold colour, and it has two or three runners about a foot long. In addition to its lovely colour and scent, it has the advantage of being suitable for cutting, as the flowers are carried on an unusually long stalk, and grow thick.

The dwarf nasturtium is ideal for bordering, and is now obtainable in great variety of colouring. I found a nasturtium with a flower that seemed poised for flight, like the lovely aquilegia. I mixed it with *Warscewicizii*, which I bought entirely for its name, on discovering it in a catalogue. I wrote the name down on a piece of paper and had enormous fun trying it on my friends. No one could pronounce it, and no one knew what it was. Some declared that no place of that name existed! An intelligent friend thought it was the name of a Polish violinist in the Nineties, and another believed it was a fortress in Galicia destroyed by the Russian army under Brusiloff in 1916. However, I do not belong to that order of gardeners who delight in stunning their visitors with an avalanche of frightful names. There's always some preposterous woman who talks about her myosotis, and thereby robs forget-me-not of half its charm. And I knew a frightful man who said his *mimulus moschatus* had died. I replied that I had had no luck with my variegated linoleum.

There are names, of course, that fascinate one.

Ever since meeting a toucan in the Zoo at Marseilles I have wanted to own one, not only for its gorgeous beak, but that I might say, "Have you seen my toucan?" Also I would like to own a pangolin, despite the fact that it might come up through the kitchen floor, as happened to a friend of mine in India.

Warscewicizii, with its scarlet flower, made an excellent border mixture with my chameleon dwarf nasturtiums. There is one other notable quality about the nasturtium. When cut for indoor decoration it retains its splendid colour and vivacity in artificial light. Some flowers lose all their lustre in electric light, but the nasturtium, even the yellow, retains its brilliance. There is also another table use for this attractive plant. Its leaves make an excellent salad, together with its seeds. Here is the recipe given me by someone who astonished me one evening with this *Salade Chaude*.

"Select large young nasturtium leaves and cut into strips. Mix with a similar amount of white lettuce. Split a tablespoonful of the seeds gathered fresh from the runners, and put nasturtium leaves and seeds and lettuce in a salad bowl. Over this pour a dressing composed of vinegar, sugar, and a little mustard, pepper and salt. The dressing should be added to the salad a few minutes only before eating."

The nasturtium has one drawback. It is the favourite edible of the green caterpillar, and the underside of the leaves must be constantly watched to check the ravages of this pest.

My garden being an inherited and not a created one, I was often surprised by its inhabitants. I would go

out one morning to see whether a monstrous cat had
again withered a patch of my lawn with its picric
micturition, and turning in my wrath from a fresh
scene of desolation I would be arrested by a strange
flower that had raised its head overnight. An energetic attempt to identify the stranger was always made,
and often it was an exasperating experience. I called
in neighbours, and waylaid professional and amateur
gardeners. Often they confessed their ignorance; too
often they didn't, and gave the exhibit a name which
proved to be wrong. Happily I had one friend almost
infallible, and I saved my doubtful flower exhibits for
his visit.

But there was an occasion when he, with all his
knowledge, was baffled, and honestly confessed it. One
morning I noticed in the border of one of my beds
a certain growth whose shape and colour filled me
with astonishment. It had pushed up through the
earth overnight, I swear. It had a thick green stalk,
slightly covered with greyish spots. There was something not quite healthy about this stranger, something
sinister, in fact. At the tip of the stalk there was a
head, undeveloped, which might be the bud of a flower,
or a sheath of leaves. I called in various persons to
look at it, but no one had ever seen such a plant before. General opinion seemed to regard it as a fungus,
but there was something too proud in its bearing for
that lowly tribe.

The days passed, the stalk grew stronger and taller.
The grey-green spots gave a leopard-like appearance
to the stranger. One morning the head and seven
leaves spread themselves out. There was no sign of

any calyx of a flower appearing. But those leaves day by day achieved a perfect symmetry.

By this time the plant was the centre of great interest. It attracted visitors anxious like myself to solve the mystery. When the plant was a foot high there was something quite sinister in its appearance. It was called a 'revolting plant' by one observer, and another named it 'the Devil's Spawn.' But all this did not solve the mystery. It was suggested that I should pot it and take it to Kew for expert examination, but there was the trouble, and also the fear that moving might kill it.

By now the mysterious growth was an object of widespread interest. Friends rang me up from London to enquire after its health. It flourished exceedingly. The seven leaves, held to be symbolic of the Seven Deadly Sins, grew and grew. There was no flower, no promise of any flower. What was the plant going to do, for all plants do something if you watch long enough. After two months' observation of the mystery I had to go abroad. The plant was now almost two feet high and the spotted stem was like a giraffe's neck. I left instructions that it was to be watched closely, and any manifestations reported to me.

I was in Paris a week later and one day went out to dine with a friend, who had just purchased a house on the edge of the Bois de Boulogne. I have two vivid memories of the Bois. It was there that I first saw Anatole France, and a Judas tree in flower. I don't know which was the more astonishing sight, the old gentleman with the long nose, or the little tree with the rose-purple blossoms. I am not disposed to hero-worship, but I did remove my hat and stand aside in the shade while an immortal passed under a tree so lovely. I was conscious of both at once, and thus seen, the legend of Judas was eclipsed, and a memory of Anatole France established. For me it is now his tree, and whenever I am in Paris in May I go to the Bois, and seek out that tree under whose blossom I first saw *le maître*.

My friend's house on the edge of the Bois possessed a small garden, but it was the garden inside the house that surprised me. His wife, it transpired, was an enthusiastic indoor gardener. They did not possess a greenhouse, but it seemed to me that everything growable in pots, with little light or space, was grown in that house.

On the whole I do not like to live in a bulbery, surrounded by bowls filled with brown fibre. There is something unnatural about this process of incubating. The greenhouse is obviously a large forcing frame, and is the laboratory of the garden. But this bowl culture is somewhat indecent. It is spying on the process of gestation, and standing by, water-jug in hand, while an 'interesting condition' becomes a happy event. "Look, they're coming!" cries an ecstatic friend, pointing to some shoots lurking in the fibre. When they do come and burst into full flower I feel sorry for those bulbs, reared in an atmosphere of food and tobacco smoke. I cannot help thinking of Keats's *Pot of Basil*. I am certain that if I probed down among those dank swaddling clothes I should exhume a corpse. I have to confess, nevertheless, that I have seen astonishingly healthy hyacinths blooming in bowls, but then I have seen the healthiest-looking children blooming in dark slums, and conversely, country children with a sickly pallor.

My hostess's bulbs were all healthy, all pushing up vigorously through the fibre. I observed that my host dropped his cigarette ash into the bowels, but there is something miraculous about cigarette ash, since friends assure me, when I look alarmed at their deposits, that it does my carpets good.

The mantelpiece in the morning-room was like a window-box with its bright array of shooting bulbs, but my attention was attracted by one large bulb that had escaped from its bowl. It sat like a withered old hag among the cheerful shoots. I asked my friend why he kept it. Was it aromatic?

"Oh, that! Haven't you seen one of those?" he asked, picking it up. "It'll break out any day now."

"Break out?" I queried, looking at the withered thing. "Mumps or scarlet fever?"

"That's not the way to talk of the Monarch of the East. Have you never seen one?"

"Never—I can't believe that'll ever do anything," I retorted.

"Then you'd better take one home and see for yourself—you'll have the surprise of your life."

A week later I departed. In the corner of my bag nestled a Monarch of the East.

"You don't think it'll burst into bloom in mid-Channel?" I asked derisively. "I'm not accustomed to travel with monarchs."

When the Customs officer asked me if I had anything

to declare, I proudly exclaimed, "Yes, a Monarch of the East."

The man looked startled. I unfolded the sad-looking bulb.

"A cousin of King Hussein," I explained.

The man touched it as if it were a bomb, put a chalk mark on my bag and left me. I put His Majesty back into the sponge bag.

At home I placed the bulb on a mantelpiece and watched it with growing scepticism. Wonders had been predicted concerning its resurrection. Even after that it was remarkable in death, I was assured. Potted and freely watered, it had a reincarnation in a changed body. As a bulb it was supposed to produce a gorgeous flower. After the death of the flower it had to be potted and watered, when it came up a plant three feet high.

I had scarcely believed a word of all this, and whenever I looked at that miserable dry bulb sitting naked on my mantelpiece I had to fight an impulse to put it to bed, poultice it with fibre and supply it with drink. It is not in my nature to keep anything without food and drink.

The days passed, and the weeks. One morning, as my servant was dusting, she gave a cry. That bulb was alive! Something was shooting out of the mummy. Immediately the bulb became the most exciting thing in my life. I almost sat up late to watch it shooting. Now that it had begun, it grew apace. One inch, two, three, four—it actually grew up a foot. And then it began to swell and we became anxious. It had already become top-heavy, and we had to fasten the bulb down.

Then one morning we rose to find the Monarch reigning in glory on the mantelpiece, a glorious sight with its flower, red-brown, tipped with red and yellow. I transferred it to my desk and sat down and wrote to my friend in the very shadow of its splendour.

After a too brief reign its glory faded, the flower shrivelled up, the bulb was only a bulb again. Anxiously I awaited the predicted sign. In a little while a growth began to come from the bulb. Straightway I potted the bulb in rich soil and watered it. Having beheld the first miracle, I was firm in my faith in a second. If my friend had assured me it would rise up in an ectoplasm satisfactory to the Society for Psychical Research, I would have believed him.

It did rise up at last, and a ghost could not have astonished me more. After the first shock I picked up the pot and hurried off to a neighbour, unable to credit my own eyes. He stared at the plant with its long stout stalk, its spotted giraffe-like neck. We agreed that a great mystery troubling us had at last been solved. This reincarnation of the Monarch of the East was the mysterious stranger in my garden the previous year! The spotted visitor was identified at last.

SUMMER LAZINESS

I have not written a word to-day,
   The sun laughed through my apple trees,
The birds had such a lot to say,
   My poplars rustled in the breeze;
"Why write, poor fool, there's nothing in it,
Be lazy!" sang a merry linnet.

Lazy I was, and yet it seems
   I have achieved much happiness
In watching how the sunlight gleams
   Through boughs of blossom that caress
The sky's blue face, in hearing birds
Sing to me songs that need not words.

Books we can make by taking thought,
   What sentence has a flower's grace?
What wisdom equals beauty taught
   By songbirds in a leafy place?
And all the things wise Plato knew
Provide less wonder than the dew.

All day I listened under boughs
   Where blossom fell and birds were calling;
Green waves of shadow swept my house
   From four slim poplars, ever falling
Down through the sunlit bowl of noon,
Upon whose rim there stole a moon.

The day slipped into dusk, the night
   Scattered a million stars in space,
The last wind slept, a bird in fright
   Twittered in some far woodland place;
One with the languid earth I went
To fold in sleep a day's content.

CHAPTER IX

MR. CHAUCER, KING CHARLES, AND THE BLACKSMITH

I

WHEN friends learn that I am the owner of three cottages they cannot resist a joke about 'the Squire.' My village is so small that ownership of half a dozen of its cottages would almost make one an autocrat. But the manner in which I became the owner of two other cottages is a story that will serve as a sad example of the passing of the English countryside.

I suppose it is a hamlet rather than a village in which I live. It possesses two inns, but one of these is on the main highway to Oxford, and does not seem to belong to us. We are indeed grateful to it, for the whole of my village hides away behind it. It is optimistically called *The Traveller's Rest*, and stands exactly at a point, after a straight mile, where motorists are 'all out' to tackle the hill behind it, while those coming down are equally 'all out' to see what they can 'touch' on the level.

The travellers seldom rest, therefore; they go past at anything from sixty to eighty miles an hour. Nor can I assert that they miss much. It is a large gabled house, flat-faced and roofy. Its drabness is relieved by two things—a well-painted sign and a well-kept garden in front. The original *Traveller's Rest*, where travellers by horse or carriage probably did rest, is across the road, and is now a picturesque private house nestling by a park wall.

The other inn, the real inn of the village, has both history and beauty. I discovered one day, almost by accident, that it is linked with romance, as we see it to-day. Mine host, Mr. Harris, an old soldier, is adept with a gun, a tankard of ale, a handful of darts, a shove-'a'penny board, a skittle ball, a tug-o'-war rope, a ferret in a bag, a car that wants 'looking at,' or anything else in which an all-round man with unfailing good nature can excel.

My admirable Mr. Harris one day gave me a start. I had been looking at *The Golden Ball*, and had come to the conclusion that it had once been a coach-stage. It has a space in front of the old taproom that suggested a former inn-yard, into which the flying coach had come for a change of horses, or for additional horse-power to tackle the old Oxford road that winds up behind. I could imagine the bustle of this inn yard, with harness rooms, and a gallery surrounding the ostlers' quarters.

The inn itself has a delightful bay window that juts out into the road, where it curves through the heart of the village. *The Golden Ball* shines gaily in the sun with its red tiles and yellow-washed walls, and seen from the surrounding hills, its shape, colour and position on the floor of the valley are altogether a perfect example of the English scene.

I had known Mr. and Mrs. Harris for three years before their bombshell was dropped on me. Keeping an ever-open door and heart, I had turned to them a hundred times in domestic emergencies. When a sudden descent of visitors for tea had used up all the bread, it was to Mrs. Harris that my servant fled for relief supplies. When a field rat attacked my larder, again it was Mr. Harris, with a ferret, 'Sally,' and his dog 'Ponto,' who delivered us from the raider. When I had a houseful, and another guest had to be 'slept,' it was Mrs. Harris who took him in. A sudden shortage of matches or candles, a breakdown in the newspaper delivery, a demand for stamps after post-office hours, *The Golden Ball* never failed me.

This readiness to help was all the more gracious because I was the inn's worst customer. I am neither a drinker nor a smoker by choice. I make the effort in sheer sociability, but I should never be aware of the absence of either of these things. There is always a smile in *The Golden Ball* at my efforts to drink beer. Any friends gifted that way I eagerly take along to make up for my deficiency. I like to sit in the parlour and hear the vanishing Oxfordshire, as opposed to the expanding Oxford, accent. You meet there men still wise in the way of horses, followers of the plough, builders of ricks, thatchers, men who seem doomed to be the last of a great line extinguished by the machine. You hear many a strange story, such as the one I have told of the cock with a wooden leg.

But for some reason I had never regarded Mr. Harris as a repository of local history. Compared with some of the Methuselahs of the village he is a mere boy, and a newcomer. The air of the sergeant, the old soldier with Indian experience, the retired Oxfordshire constable, redoubtable in the tug-of-war, stills hangs about him, for all his handiness with a beer-pump or spade.

I mentioned my suspicions about the coach-stage. It was as if I had touched a spring. All I had surmised was correct. He showed me the place where the incoming mail coach from Aylesbury to Henley turned in, also the 'Tantivy' from Birmingham, a red coach; the 'Magnet' from Cheltenham, a blue; the 'Alert' from Oxford, and the Gloucester and the Stroud Mails. "No wonder Tom King and Dick Turpin hung about here," said Mr. Harris.

He was building a hen coop at that moment, and I was glad he did not see my face. Astonishment quickly changed to incredulity. Of course this was the kind of local yarn one might expect. Dick Turpin was a hero of mine at seven. I can recall now the sore place on my thumb made by a pair of scissors, and the mess of gum on my fingers and clothes. My father had returned one day with a large coloured cardboard sheet on which was painted the wonderful pictorial history of Dick Turpin's great ride to York. I worked feverishly by night, cutting out and pasting up on the plan the toll-gate, the astonished keeper, the six-barred gate, the leaping horse, and the great Dick going over it, masked, with pistol cocked. There was rebellion when I had to go to bed without the toll-house's roof on. Waking early I descended through a sleeping house, and in a cold room returned to the scissors and the gum pot. Oh, that ecstasy of childhood, evoked by coloured cardboard and gallant, defiant Dick!

Dick Turpin had ridden to York along the Great North Road. I could not believe that brave Black Bess had cantered past my garden, or that, booted and spurred, the highwayman had darkened the threshold of *The Golden Ball*.

"Haven't you seen his hiding-place?" asked Mr. Harris, driving home a nail.

"No," I answered, and added, half in protest, "but Turpin couldn't have been here—he was on the Great North Road!"

"Well, he was born in Essex and worked all round London. He knew every inch of the Chilterns. He'd places to dive in when it got hot for him. Come and have a look, sir."

I followed Mr. Harris, determined not to be led away by the mere thirst for romance. Dick Turpin in my own village! It was fantastic.

The old ostlers' taproom is now a private living-room, but in the old days it communicated with the parlour for the gentry. Between these two rooms there is a thick chimney-stack. As is usual with these old chimneys there is a bend in it. This bend had been completely hidden by boarding. To my surprise Mr. Harris opened a cupboard door, revealing a narrow staircase leading to a bedroom above. There was also a space in the bend for a man to stand and look down through a slit at all the occupants of the bar. The ingenuity and secrecy of this place were obviously designed to assist a hunted man. There was a main staircase to the room above. It was easy, while the officers of the Law were searching the house, for the occupant of the upstairs room to slip out by the hidden staircase, and observe from his secret place of vantage the movements in the bar below him. Further enquiries elicited the fact that Turpin and King had 'worked' the Oxford and Watlington roads. Mr. Harris's exciting news was largely confirmed.

Within a week I had a second shock. At that time I was employing an old gardener. He was so old, he was counting up the eighties, that he could not go up a ladder because of dizziness, kneel because of rheumatism or dig because of lumbago. He had been born in the village, as had his forebears. He had spent his pennies, he told me, in my drawing-room, when it was a sweetshop, and had seen my tall poplars arrive on a handbarrow. One day I asked him what he had done with the grass from the lawn mower.

"I've put it on the Roman road," he said.

"The *what?*" I cried, jumping out of my skin.

"The Roman road, sir."

"Where is the Roman road?"

"Why, this lane, sir. It was the Oxford road when I was a boy, but we always called it the Roman road."

"Who's *we?*"

"Oh, everybody. My dad and my grandad always called it the Roman road. It was the way them Romans walked to Dorchester. They came over by the ford at Henley and up Friday Street and down the Mile, and along 'ere and up the hill where this lane runs into the new Oxford road again. I've 'eard my grandad say as 'is grandad said that Mr. Chaucer, the King's poet, used to walk this way. And King Charles, when he was skeered out of Oxford, came down 'ere and went up into them woods to avoid Henley, where they was waiting for 'im. An' 'e 'ad a friend up at Fawley Court, who was now against 'im, but 'e winked

and let King Charles go by. Ev course, I've only
'eard this and none of us was scholars."

I let the old man go on, though my head was reeling
and a hundred questions came to my lips. When he
had finished, and started clipping again, I went straight
into the house to keep calm. There were certain head-
lines to this astonishing information. My lane was
a Roman road before it was the old Oxford road.
"Mr." Chaucer had walked along it. King Charles
had fled down it.

I have heard that local tradition is often more trust-
worthy than the written word. My gardener was
eighty-five. The recollections of his grandfather, allowing three generations of eighty years each, would
take us back to around 1740. The grandfather's
grandfather, therefore, might well have been living in
the village on the day King Charles fled through it.
It should not be difficult to find whether the King had
come this way. That he had been at Henley and Oxford, I knew. It seemed probable he might have
journeyed this way, by the hedge of my garden. But
I wanted to pursue the Chaucer trail. Charles could
wait.

I returned to the garden, and found something to do
by the hedge where the old man was clipping.

"I suppose," I said, casually, "Mr. Chaucer was on
his way to Oxford when he went past here?"

The old man stopped clipping.

"Not at all, sir. 'E was going to visit 'is son at
Ewelme."

"Ewelme?"

"It's about ten miles from 'ere, sir, just off the

Oxford road. Mr. Chaucer's son's buried there, where old Henry VIII 'ad 'is 'oney-moon—one of 'em. My grandad said the poet was very fond of the country. 'E wrote a lot about it, an' 'e was a bit bawdy, too."

I had heard this criticism before, but I had never expected to hear it from a gardener. My curiosity was aroused. I had not seen Ewelme. That afternoon I went to Ewelme.

I have not yet recovered from the fact that for three years I lived near to anything so lovely and surprising without discovering it. Surely it is one of the loveliest old churches in England? It has a battlemented exterior, a gargoyled tower, and an alms chapel added about 1437. An almshouse for thirteen old men is reached through an archway of moulded brick, and the cloister of these almshouses has uprights of black timber with herringbone brick between them. All the bedrooms have dormer windows with a sitting-room below each. Nearby there is a school, also of Tudor brick, with square-headed stone-mullioned windows and rectangular dripstones. This noble group of buildings clings to the hillside, with the village and its watercress-bed below.

But it was concerning Mr. Chaucer that I had come hither, so I hurried on into the church. I must not digress, though sorely tempted. I could write pages about the roofs. The chapel roof is of beautifully carved Spanish chestnut, and, as the beetle cannot attack the wood, it has never been restored since the early fifteenth century. There is a carved font cover, with the Tudor rose on its counterpoise, four diminishing tiers of arches, and a richly crocketed spire with the figure of St. Michael on top. There are fantastically carved corbels and fifteenth-century brasses.

Yet it is the tombs that make this church so rich in interest. That of the Duchess of Suffolk is a masterpiece. She has a ducal coronet on her head, and the Garter on her left forearm. Over her head is a canopy carved from a single block of alabaster. In the open space below the tomb—the Sexton supplies a cushion and loves to make you go down on your hands and knees—there is a gruesome emaciated figure of the Duchess in death. This lady married, first, Thomas Montacute, Earl of Salisbury, killed at Orleans in 1428; and secondly the Duke of Suffolk, who was murdered. His father was killed at Agincourt, but lies here, for his body was boiled and brought to England.

Now this Duchess, so lovely above and so gruesome below her tomb, was Alice Chaucer. And this Alice Chaucer was the daughter of the Thomas Chaucer whose tomb lies nearby. Duke John gave to the church his mother's, the Duchess's tomb, the font cover and the shields on the tomb of Thomas Chaucer, his grandfather. And this Thomas Chaucer, who died in 1434, was the son of Mr. Chaucer the poet.

The facts, therefore, so far as the records in this church go, are not incompatible with my gardener's astonishing story. He had heard it from his great-great-grandfather viâ his grandfather. That was getting well back into history. It is almost safe to assume these ancestors were 'illiterate,' which meant they relied on hearsay. They had not read about King Charles or Mr. Chaucer or the Roman road. The legacy of oral tradition accounts for their knowledge. They would not invent the story of the Roman road, or of Mr. Chaucer going to visit his son at Ewelme, or of King Charles's flight through the village.

In the matter of King Charles the First I was soon able to confirm the legend by the strict historical fact. King Charles fled from Oxford on the 27th April, 1646. Disguised as a groom, accompanied by John Ashburnham and Dr. Hudson, he rode towards Henley to avoid the town, then in the hands of the Parliamentarians. He turned aside at the end of the Fairmile, and went by a bridle-path through Henley Park, and slept that night at Hambledon Manor. The friend who 'winked,' according to my gardener, and let him go by, was Sir Bulstrode Whitelock, living at Fawley Court.

It seems beyond doubt, therefore, that Charles the First passed the end of my garden on the 27th April, 1646, and saw the chimney-stack and the red-tiled roof exactly as I see them now. There is another link in the cottage itself. On a wall there hangs a portrait, by Van Dyck, of Henrietta of France, his Bourbon Queen, whose obdurate nature sustained the King in his fatal course. Now, in a room not twenty yards from her royal husband's track, the Queen looks down the centuries.

It happens, too, that I have a certain family interest in this Mr. Chaucer who went along my lane to Ewelme, if the gardener's legend is true. There was a certain John Roberts who was of some importance in his day. He became secretary to Henry Pelham, a Prime Minister and the ingenious originator of 'Consols.' When this John Roberts died, fat with sinecures, his children erected a monument in Westminster Abbey, and part of Chaucer's tomb was removed to make room for it, a piece of effrontery somewhat redeemed by the real beauty of the monument itself. But I never see it without feeling slightly ashamed of my ancestors, and apologetic towards the excellent though bawdy Mr. Chaucer.

My interest aroused by the gardener's reminiscences, I looked up the facts concerning Bulstrode Whitelock, who had so obligingly 'winked' at his friend. Everything I discovered confirmed my gardener's statement. By one of those coincidences rarely allowed to the novelist, though common enough in life, I had that week received for review a 'Life' of Christina, Queen of Sweden.

Whitelock was sent as Ambassador by Cromwell to effect a trade alliance with Sweden. At the time of his arrival at her Court she had already made plans to abdicate the throne, at a considerable price, and settle in Rome. There she became a Catholic, to the rage and consternation of Protestant Sweden, kept a salon, turned the head of a Cardinal, and in turn courted and flouted the Pope. "I have known four Popes, not one of whom had common sense," wrote the intrepid lady.

But at the time of Whitelock's arrival in 1653, no one, except the Queen, dreamed of the Roman adventure. She took a liking to the pompous Ambassador. He was conceited, but she saw that he was as shrewd as he was vain. In his first meeting he extolled her line for its defence of the Protestant cause. Coming from a land that had beheaded its King, he had much to overcome, but he gained her confidence. He found also that she was acquisitive.

"What huge dog is this?" she demanded.

"It is an English mastiff, which I brought with me. It seems it is broke loose, and followed me even to this place."

"Is he gentle and well-conditioned?" she asked.

"The more courage they have," said Whitelock, "the more gentle they are; this is both. Your Majesty may stroke him."

Her Majesty stroked him, and Whitelock therefore made her a present of the dog. I like to fancy that the English mastiff raced in these fields around me before going to the Swedish Court.

Whitelock was soon to learn the cost of the Queen's admiration. She had seen the horses he had brought from England, and greatly admired them. One day, discussing hunting, she said she thought of sending to England for a horse. It was a hint that could not be ignored. She was offered and accepted a present of three of his horses.

Gradually he gained her favour. Then one day she took him aside. "I have great confidence in your honour and judgment, and therefore, though you are a stranger, I shall acquaint you with a business of the greatest consequence to me in the world." She then informed the astonished Whitelock of her intention to abdicate. After he had implored her not to take this momentous step his shrewdness asserted itself.

"Madame, let me humbly advise you, if any such thing should be, as I hope it will not, to reserve that country in your possession out of which your reserved revenue shall be issued; for when money is to be paid out of a prince's treasury, it is not always ready and certain."

This warning proved prophetic, even though the Queen followed his advice.

Twenty years later, after various changes of fortune, Whitelock was buried at Fawley, in the churchyard that lies on the plateau some three hundred and fifty feet above my cottage. In 1632 he had erected in the church a fine monument to his father and mother, the figures under a canopy supported by black marble columns is still in fine preservation.

II

Following the gardener's story of the man who winked when his King was escaping, I went up to Fawley Church to look at the monument. What little causes lead to momentous occasions! This visit was to enrich me with a rare friendship, and make me a local landlord.

It was a lovely late October day when I visited the church. The Whitelock monument proved much finer than I had anticipated. As I passed through the churchyard I lingered for a few moments before a memorial cross that had been draped with the Union Jack. The base of this village memorial to those fallen in the Great War was covered with floral tributes.

While looking at these I became aware of a little old lady who had been tending the flowers. We entered into a conversation, and presently I was conscious of having encountered a remarkable and charming personality. What vivacity in this old lady with apple-rosy cheeks and bright blue eyes! She possessed a natural courtesy in speech and gesture that grew upon one. Gradually I learned the personal tragedy that brought her into the churchyard. She had just placed some flowers to commemorate the death of her only son the last month of the War. When I told her I knew the battlefield where he had fallen, that at the time I must have been very near, and that even now on my cottage wall there hung the map of that battle-field with the regiments involved listed with Haig's own hand on the margin, a bond drew us together in its solemn memory.

She invited me to her cottage, which possessed a great view over the Thames Valley as far as a ridge on which Windsor Castle might be discerned, and the Hog's Back in Surrey. Gradually she unfolded much local history, with her own. Her husband was the late vil-lage blacksmith. He was eighty-four, she was seventy-six. For fifty years he had rung the church-bells. For over three hundred years his forefathers had lain in this same churchyard. And now the last of the line lay in Flanders.

Presently we came to the village green. Some dis-tance back from it stood a triple gabled cottage. You approached it down a garden path lined, at this late season, with dahlias, fuchsias, Michaelmas daisies, and chrysanthemums. It was the village blacksmith's cot-tage of one's dream.

On one side of the garden stood the smithy. I looked inside. The sight smote the heart. No fire leapt in the forge. The bellows were thick in dust, the windows and rafters were hung with clusters of cobwebs. The benches were still littered with a black-smith's tools. Horseshoes lay around, with boxes of nails, rusted hammers and pincers, and a great anvil. I thought—who could help it?—of the poem of the Village Blacksmith. Here was no spreading chestnut tree, but at this door on the village green generations of schoolchildren had looked in to see the sparks fly, the fire glow and hear the anvil ring. Here once upon a time eighty horses had been shod in a week, and the blacksmith had risen early to ply his craft. Now no horses come, the smithy is falling into ruin, for the horse is becoming a curiosity.

My new friend invited me in to meet the blacksmith. He was sitting in a long oak-beamed room, with pleasant views on either side, and a wide oven-fireplace on whose hob the kettle sang. Across his knees rested the largest cat I have ever seen, which he displaced as he rose to greet me. The blacksmith? Surely it was a bishop who bade me welcome, so noble this face with its silver beard, and age-bent figure in neat black. I took the proffered chair, and little by little the saga of village life was unfolded for me. Then, at my elbow I found a tray. My hostess was entreating me to have a glass of home-made wine and a biscuit.

That was the beginning of many visits, of a quickly ripening friendship with this grand old couple. Here they sat quietly in the evening of their lives observing the changes around. The position of the village had helped to preserve it from the inroads of a restless age. It was still a village in which there was neither electric

light nor gas. More surprising, even in a village without an inn or a shop, there was not even water. Situated at a height of nearly five hundred feet above sea-
level, on a crest of the Chilterns, the village was
completely isolated, although it was less than forty
miles from London.

From the blacksmith's window one looked across the
three-acre field behind the house on to a panorama of
the Berkshire hills. Immediately below, the glorious
beechwoods of this district swept down to the Thames
below Henley. The isolation of the village had been
preserved by the fact that it belonged to a large estate,
owned at one time by the Bulstrode Whitelock who
had winked at his King's escape. In the subsequent
changes of ownership the estate had been preserved
almost intact. The blacksmith's life, as that of most
of the inhabitants of this village, had been bound up
with that of the Squire, whose doings at the 'Court'
were still the chief topic of interest among the ancients.

A long drought during the summer had inspired the
Press to an outcry on the scandal of village water
supplies. But I found the blacksmith and his wife
not at all inclined to be indignant. They had been
drinking rain-water for sixty years, water collected
in an underground tank from the roof. There had
been no ill results in all those years, and many people,
observing the sprightliness of my two friends, would
begin to wonder whether there were not medicinal
virtues in water straight from Heaven instead of from
the waterworks, through fifty miles of pipes.

Some thirty years back the village had been excited
by the sinking of a common well on the green. It en-

tailed the sinking of a shaft three hundred and fifty feet deep before water was struck, and the excitement evoked by this task was crowned by an escapade of the Squire's daughter. She descended the shaft with some friends and was held to ransom for a round of beer by the workmen she joined at the bottom.

The countryman is not a lover of innovations. The well was soon neglected, like the village hall erected in a fever of war-memorialism. The chief criticism of the well was voiced by one of the greybeards who watched the gigantic digging operations with frank disapproval. "Ay, they're keen enough to get down to the watter; they'll not be so keen to get it up!" The Methuselahs were right. Only in the direst scarcity does the village send the bucket to the well. The incongruities of our civilisation could scarcely be better illustrated than by this instance of a village, which, one hour by road from London, in telephone communication with New York or any capital in Europe, and nightly listening to music in Paris, Berlin or Rome, lacks a single tap, bath or lavatory among fifty cottage inhabitants!

But at the time of my intrusion great changes, some of them lamentable, were impending. It became a pleasant habit for me and my guests to make a walking excursion to the village blacksmith's. His wife was an avid and intelligent reader, and I generally arrived with a new book. In the winter we walked through the dusk of the short afternoon, with the smell of the wet earth and the keen wind in our nostrils. With what eager welcome the cottage door flew open, the fire was poked, the cat turned out of the best chair, the lamp lit and tea laid on the table! I have arrived there, fresh from London, Paris or Berlin, from a sophisticated world in which new inventions for man's murder were acclaimed side by side with new schemes for preventing man's bankruptcy. Entering that snug parlour, and confronting those kind faces, lovely in honourable age, I have wondered whether we have not lost something even more valuable than a gold standard. For the blacksmith's race has gone for ever from the earth.

There are other excellencies, since character can triumph over most conditions, but there will be never again just this kind of tranquillity and honest worth. Generations, living simply, observing the seasons, self-reliant in work and pleasure, have bred the blacksmith's type. There will be a day when we shall try to revert to this type, but it will be in vain. The smithy will have changed to a garage on the village green, the lanes will all be straightened for motor-cars, the land cut up for speculative building, the old cottages renovated for week-enders. We cannot stay the hand of Time. In visiting the blacksmith and his wife I feel I am enjoying an epoch that already belongs to History.

In the long room of the cottage, by the chimney corner, Mark Harman sits in a highbacked arm-chair with wings. That chair was given him by the village in celebration of fifty years of bell-ringing in the church. The presentation was an event in village life. The Squire was in the chair, and an even older contemporary was also the recipient of a similar chair. Old Charlie Sharp was eighty-five, Mark Harman was eighty-three, and James Rixon, the baby, of whom more anon, aged eighty, was also present. The Squire alluded to the fact that the first Sharp appeared in the registers in 1578 and the first Harman in 1668, and these two old bell-ringers represented the last in male descent of their line.

Unhappily the blacksmith and his wife were not present through illness, so off went a deputation of villagers to present Mr. Harman with the chair, and an illuminated address. The cottage room was crowded with beaming faces and rang with the "Hear! Hear!" of the chairman's supporters. Nor must I omit mention of the cake. This had been specially made in celebration of the event, and its shape accorded a fitting compliment to the two bell-ringers. It was in the form of a church bell, of chocolate colour, with a piece of rope in almond paste hanging from the top. The sides of the bell were adorned with wreaths of flowers done in sugar of various colours and with the names of Mark and Charlie. "It was very much admired of all," says the local chronicle.

It is in this grandfather chair, presented to him by the villagers, that I often find the blacksmith nursing the gigantic cat. He is not so active as his wife, complains at moments of dizziness, but never fails in the fine points of hospitality. Sometimes I surprise him in the old smithy, where he will retire on a summer day to muse on past labours, but it is in the winter evenings, with the round lamp glowing on the table, and the fire burning brightly in the grate, that he looks more patriarchal. There is almost a ritual before our departure.

"You'll have a glass of wine, sir—home-made?" asks Mrs. Harman.

"Thank you very much, but I don't think so," I reply.

"Just a glass, sir—it will keep you warm."

I look at Louis, who is with me; he looks at me.

"You know, Mrs. Harman, it makes us sing all the way home," he confesses.

"I can't think what the villagers will think when they see us staggering out of your cottage," I add.

"Well, there's a full moon to-night," says the blacksmith with a chuckle. "You'll find your way back."

Meanwhile Mrs. Harman has disappeared. She returns with a tray on which there are two wine-glasses and a bottle. She fills the glasses. The wine is the old lady's parsnip brew. A tin of biscuits is opened. We drink the health of the old couple. The wine, as ever, is potent.

It is time to go. We firmly prevent our host rising from his chair. Our hostess escorts us to the door, and despite our protests insists on seeing us down the path to the gate. She waits in the lighted doorway until we have crossed the village green. We look back, and our last glimpse is of a low cottage, grey under a bright full moon. The windows glow yellow, in the doorway the lamplight silhouettes a silver-headed figure. With a last 'Good night' the door closes.

We take the moonlit road that winds along the ridge of the Chilterns; the woods in the far valley are blanketed with mist. Do we sway a little? Louis bursts into song. I join him.

Parlez-moi d'amour, redites-moi des choses tendres,
Votre beau discours mon cœur n'est pas las de l'entendre
Pourvu que toujours vous répétiez ces mots suprêmes,
Je vous aime.

"Louis, this is disgraceful!" I protest, breaking off.

"No, *mon cher,* we are young."

"We are drunk—and on parsnip wine!"

"It is a vair lovely night," asserts Louis. "They are charming. I like England greatly. We have reason to sing. *Quelle belle nuit!* Look!"

We stare for a few moments where a leafless tree throws a lacework of jet on the white road. Through the still night comes the rumble of a train in the far valley. An owl hoots. The beauty of it all silences us. Later, as my cottage glimmers at the foot of the steep road, Louis says—"You must ask Mrs. Harman for the recipe of her wine. I will take it to France."

I did. I copy the recipe from the sheet she gave me, covered with that fine Italian-point writing our grandmothers learned, a legacy from far-off Elizabethan days when our culture was Italian.

Mrs. Harman's Recipe for Parsnip Wine

Wine made of the parsnip root approaches nearer to the Malmsey of Madeira and the Canaries than any other wine; it is made with little expense or trouble, and only requires to be kept a few years to be made as agreeable to the palate as it is wholesome to the body.

To every 5 lb. of parsnips pared and cut up as for table, put 1 gallon of water; boil them till they are quite tender; drain them through a sieve, but do not bruise them, as no remedy would clear afterwards. Pour the liquor into a pan and to each gallon add 4 lb. of Demerara sugar, stirring well to dissolve sugar.

When luke warm add 1 oz. of yeast; after 3 days it should be put into a stone bottle; keep the bottle filled up as it ferments over; when it ceases, cork the bottle down. March or September is the proper season for making it.

To improve flavour I put the rind and juice of 2 lemons and 3 Seville oranges to every gallon and boil it with the parsnips.

And that's what makes you sing!

THE VILLAGE BLACKSMITH

(New version to the tune of "Bonnie Dundee")

In his chair in the evening, the cat on his knees,
The winter wind roaring and shaking the trees,
Sits Mark, the old blacksmith, his feet on the fender,
And would not change place with a king in his splen-
dour.

There are no horses come to the smithy for shoeing,
The village is buzzing with wonders a-doing,
There's light and there's power both coming by cable,
There aren't any wonders of which they're not able.

The newspaper says there's a war in the offin',
They've unearthed an old Sultan with jewels in his coffin,
The Prime Minister says there's a serious crisis:
And two boys who went skating have been drowned in
the Isis.

But Mark in his chair has a comfortable feeling
His corner is safe though the whole world is reeling;
There sits his wife sewing, God bless her dear head.
Soon she'll take a hot-bottle and place in their bed!

Yes, Mark is content,—when a man's eighty-five
He's settled the reason for keeping alive,
He's a wife still to love him, in the grate a live coal,
Good food in his stomach, and peace in his soul.

CHAPTER X

I

THERE is a firm belief, held by those who have no experience, that one has plenty of time to do things in the country. "I suppose you do all your writing there?" says someone to me when I mention Pilgrim Cottage. "On the contrary, I generally come to London to get anything done," I reply.

I am never quite believed, and a catechism follows.

"Whatever do you do then?"

"All the things that prevent me from doing the one thing I don't want to do—that's why the country's so disastrous for me. You see, I detest writing, while doing it. When it's finished one has a grand feeling."

"How very odd—I should love to write if I could," murmured my friend.

"Not at all. It would be very odd if you could, and did!"

A cloud settles on his face.

"Let me explain," I proceed, filling the sherry glasses. "The basis of my attitude is fear. I'm terrified of the new book. A moment comes when the idea obsessing me has to be pinned down with words. A whole new world has to be conceived, and lived in, to the exclusion of everything else. Unhappily,

185

I'm not one of those authors who are perfect trade-unionists, I can't insist on a day of fixed hours, and strike against overtime. It's no use, as the clock strikes noon, and I've brought Mr. Brown to the crisis of his life, my throwing down the pen and going out to mow the lawn. When I come back it would be quite unlikely that either Mr. Brown, once so vivid, or his crisis, then so imminent, would any more exist. I can't help resenting the fact that an author is allowed no private life, no time exclusively his own. His characters can walk in on him, improperly dressed if they wish. They will drag him into a conversation that lasts long after midnight. They have no scruples about keeping meals waiting even at the cost of an excellent cook. That's why I fight against this obsession and seize on any odd job to preserve my freedom. Country life provides the perfect odd-job pastime. You need never be without work to prevent work."

Sometimes walking round my cottage I wonder how many books and how much income it has cost me. Not that I regret a book unwritten or a shilling un-earned. And to be quite honest this cottage has bought itself twice in eighteen months with the ideas it has put into my head. But there is not a room in the house nor a corner in the garden where I have not done something with enormous and clumsy industry. I could have called in professional help and have had the job done with twice the speed and efficiency, and one-quarter the cost considering the amount sacrificed by neglecting my own work. But I do not regret a page unwritten, a pound unearned, or a finger blood-blistered in the joy of turning joiner, engineer or builder.

I do not see why we should hesitate to play with wood and bricks when we do not hesitate to play with garden beds and wireless sets. The two days that I turned bricklayer I count among the major pleasures of my life. Those hours of spilling mortar and tapping bricks gave me complete happiness. Unlike many other pleasures the happiness still endures, for I cured an appalling draught.

In the study stands a bookcase containing the fifteen books I have written. A charming publisher has conceived the pleasant custom each Christmas of presenting me with my latest book bound in leather by that superb artist, Sangorski. Considering their appearance, and the rewards in friendship and independence those books have brought me, I might point to them with pardonable satisfaction. But I do not. I keep them slightly obscure on a lower shelf, and it is to the fireplace that I point with bursting pride. I built it with my own hands. Let me be fair. We built it, we being Louis Tissier and myself.

A draught, like an overdraught, can menace one's domestic bliss. When the first cold snap threatened us in our cottage I complained of cold feet. In vain I piled coal and logs on to the fire, and irritably made sallies into the kitchen to know why the radiators were not hotter. That is a question I never ask now, it is useless. When the temperature falls the fire in the kitchen boiler falls, and conversely, a warm day seems to necessitate tremendous stoking. With a snowfall the fire goes out. But I am dumb, recalling my

mother's reproof when I was very young—"If servants
were intelligent, how long do you think they'd be
servants?" a question covering the whole terrain between Education Acts and Registry Offices.

Nothing cured that frightful draught. I discovered
it was caused by that infallible draught-maker, an
L-shaped room. The cold air came sweeping round the
corner into the warmer half, chilling the feet and
ankles. The bigger the fire the bigger the draught in
that immense open fireplace up which I could see the
stars. Whenever I proposed building up the fireplace
and putting in a modern front there were outcries from
my friends, who never came in winter. Surely an
Elizabethan fireplace was the chief feature in an Elizabethan house, they asked. That may be so, but unlike
Queen Elizabeth and her subjects I could not burn
whole tree-trunks or sit wrapped up in furs. Moreover, near the low ceiling the temperature was 75° Fahr.
On the floor it was around 50°.

Our thermometers call 55° temperate. Only an
animal can exist in comfort at that temperature, and
dogs and cats dislike it. A friend of mine who has
made three expeditions to the Arctic assures me the
Esquimaux live in a temperature of 90°, and are especially pleased if they can get their igloos hotter, and
sit in a blissful state of nudity. This bears out
my theory that one can only be warm in a very cold
country, such as America, Germany or Switzerland,
which is organised against the cold. The Riviera and
Italy are often like refrigerators during the cold
months.

During my first spring in the cottage I went to

Scotland to lecture for the English Association. There was a cold snap and I shivered at the prospect. Arriving at Edinburgh I chose one of the largest hotels, to ensure proper warmth. To my amazement the reception clerk informed me there was no steam heating in the bedrooms, though the reception-rooms were suffocating.

"But there are a few rooms with electric fires," he said, hopefully.

"Then give me one."

There followed a search in the register.

"I'm sorry, we have no single rooms with fires."

"Then give me a double room with a double fire," I demanded.

After another long search the clerk looked at me pitifully.

"I'll have to give you the Bridal Suite—it's the only one vacant."

The porter led me, brideless, to my suite. He unlocked a door, ushered me through a lobby, and switched on the light. I found myself in an enormous room, with two shrunken beds on a dais. "The bathroom," said the proud porter, opening another door. I passed into a white-tiled chamber with a cold glazed bath in the far corner. It looked like a refrigerator in Smithfield Market. The porter closed a window with a long pole, and disappeared. I turned to the fireplace.

It was a large Gothic affair, modelled on a baronial castle type. The bed could have been made in it. Down in front of the gigantic basket grate was an electric fire with three bars. It would take a month for that fire to warm the walls, but hopefully I stooped to put a shilling in the slot, an icy wind smiting me down the chimney. It occurred to me then that any heat generated by my shilling would only go up the chimney. So I decided to transport the fire across the room and undress near the bed. Fortunately it had a long cable.

I could not have been the first with this idea. Bridegrooms or others must have had a similar inspiration, for when I tried to move the fire I found myself frustrated. The portable electric fire had been chained to the grate behind!

There was nothing else but to undress in front of the fire, and as a protection against the arctic passage to bed I put my fur coat over my pyjamas. The iciness of the bed froze my courage. I tightened my coat around me and got into bed with it, thus surviving till morning, when I hurriedly departed.

The prospect before me was worse. I was going to Aberdeen, still farther north, to stay with a Professor at the University where I was lecturing. My courage sank to zero at thought of the windswept granite city. But on arrival at my host's a warmth smote me the moment I entered the hall that vividly recalled some American house or hotel, so adequate and pervading was it. Seldom have I seen such large steam pipes, or so many. But this was not all. In my room there were not only pipes, but also a large fire burning brightly in the grate, with a full coal-scuttle by the kerb. And when, my mission completed, I retired for the night, the kind old Professor followed me in, gave a glance at the full scuttle and said, "Keep your fire in, ye'll find it verra cold in the night!"

And as I lay in complete comfort, watching the fire-light flickering on the ceiling, I had a memory of other days when I had a fire in the bedroom by night, far off, happy days of childhood and measles.

The draught in my study had to be cured. I could not change the shape of this room. It remained for the fireplace to be reduced in size. I was as reluctant as others to lose the open fireplace, so I effected a compromise by closing in the chimney with a zinc sheet and placing a modern stove in the fireplace. It was successful but hideous. The whole character of the room was changed. I took it out. What next?

A builder brought me a book of sample fireplaces. They all looked like those lesser baronial halls that border our arterial roads, erected from a mould. Gradually I realised that my fireplace, to suit the weather-warp of the old house, would have to be slightly crude. Regularity of design would appear incongruous in a place that lacks a single straight wall or level floor.

"We must build it ourselves," said Louis, "then it will look funny."

"Funny?" I protested.

"Peculiar—is that how you say it?"

"Antique," I answered severely.

The plan was soon settled. My chimney made a sudden swerve to the left three feet up. The front wall also curved in. We decided to build the chimney of the new fireplace up until it met the old chimney. That settled, we had to find bricks and mortar. A bag of cement seemed simpler, so we bought cement at a builder's yard, where a bewildering choice of bricks met our gaze. As I looked at these bricks, large, small, oblong, square, oval and round-cornered, I experienced an ambition to build a house. I had no idea bricks could be such fascinating things, or have such delightful colours. There were blue, black, yellow, green, grey, brown, orange and white bricks. I was tempted to buy a ton, shuffle them like dominoes and build a garden house.

Finally I bought a small, sand-faced red brick, a kind of baby among the grown-ups. And here I triumphed as an amateur architect, for the first and last time. I assessed the number so accurately that when the job was finished only six bricks were left over.

The idea for the fireplace was simple. It had to be built inside the large one, reducing it to half. There was to be a small ledge where the fireplace ended and the face of the chimney began. This would leave two large gaps on either side of the new fireplace in which logs could be stored.

The bricks arrived. We began to work feverishly. The two supporting walls went up. We intended to build them straight, but they went 'funny' or 'antique' naturally. Then came the need of the cross-piece to support the chimney. We decided this must be of iron, so while Louis mixed the cement, I went off in search of a bar of iron. I visited all my neighbours' dumps and outhouses. Finally I found the side rail of an iron bed. Cut, this was the very thing. Alas, it took me two hours to cut through that rail, and I raised three blisters!

I have explained elsewhere that Louis is French. He has the Gallic temperament. Whenever we embarked on any task togther we always had a violent quarrel half-way through, in the best tradition of French comedy. But as we knew so well what would happen we arrived at a working code. At the point at which Louis threw down his tools and walked away, saying I could finish it myself, it was agreed that I should stop arguing and walk away also. Neither of us was to make the slightest reference to the incident on the resumption of work, but the one who left first should not return until the other had begun work.

As foreseen, within two hours of the start we had the first explosion. It arose from the cement. We had no knowledge that pure cement was unworkable. It almost set on the trowel. Again and again Louis would just get the stuff on to his brick only to find it was hard and intractable. Under protest I added more water and mixed the cement thinner, whereupon it ran down his arm. I laughed, and he downed tools after a grand scene. Operations were suspended for half an hour, during which time he pumped up his cycle tyre and I went to the post-office to buy stamps.

Later we resumed work, and the fireplace grew rapidly. But a moment of difficulty arrived. The new chimney had to be sealed to the old. There was no other way except for one of us to get up inside the chimney and the other to pass up the bricks and mortar. As it was dark a lighted candle had to be stuck on a ledge high up in the chimney.

At first we were defeated. The problem of Santa Claus was now ours. The passage was just too narrow for our bodies. In despair we looked at each other. It was six o'clock. In our excitement, hoping to finish the fireplace in time for an evening fire, we had gone without tea and hurried through lunch. I had even earmarked a bottle of Château-Laffitte to mark the occasion. What now? Had we to pull the whole thing down, and admit defeat?

"We can't pull it down," said Louis, grimly. "That cement's set. You'll have to dynamite the thing."

Another long silence. Then a slow smile spread over my friend's face.

"Wait!" he said enigmatically, and disappeared.

I waited, wondering what plan he had devised. Several minutes passed, and as he did not return I went into the dining-room and shouted for him.

To my surprise he answered from upstairs. Whatever was he doing up there—not breaking into the chimney from the top? No, there was not a sound. During this interval the housekeeper and the cat arrived to inspect the work.

"But it's crooked, sir!"

"We want it like that."

"Do you think it looks nice?"

Her question answered itself without any doubt as to her opinion.

"It's not finished yet," I replied, very obviously.

The cat walked into the fireplace, smelt the bricks, sneezed at the fallen soot, gave a derisive smirk and whisked away.

"Do you think it'll throw out a good heat, sir?"

"Isn't there someone at the door?" I asked desperately.

She went off, following the cat. I felt I could not endure another question. But her departing act was to draw a finger along the top of my desk and say vapidly, "The dust!"

That housekeepeer was always saying "The dust!" though she seldom dusted. "Old houses make dust," she often exclaimed. "What a lot of dust he brings in," she complained of the cat. "That coal's all dust," she would murmur when I asked for a fresh scuttleful. "I'm sure it's no use dusting," was her daily whine. She certainly had an eye for dust. She complained twice a week of a bit in her eyes. It was all the dust I ever saw her remove.

One day, when the whine was louder than ever, I remarked, cryptically, "You should have been an archæologist," but it was lost upon her; she took it for a compliment. After twelve months' endurance, enraged by the dirt I discovered under the carpets and the cushions, I treated her to a dust-storm. It was Louis who opened my eyes to the scandalous treatment I was receiving. So we took out carpets and cushions on to the lawn and very demonstratively beat them. But it did not shame her. She shut the kitchen window with a slam and gave us sponge-cake smothered in custard for a sweet. Before she finally departed a piece of kitchen ceiling fell upon her, covering her with dust. I felt it was a judgment.

My charming friend Eda, who visits me and showers advice, always good and invariably taken, said, "She must really go. That woman's imposing on you. She's lazy and dirty."

"But she complains of the dust!" I replied.

"Dust!" retorted Eda. "I've just looked under your beds. There's so much dirt there you could plant bulbs. Get rid of her!"

"But housekeepers are so difficult to find."

"Not at all," replied Eda. "Not for young bachelors. You've only to advertise and say 'A gentleman requires a Working Housekeeper to take Sole Charge of Cottage' and you'll have a hundred replies. Fifty from women who hope to marry you and fifty from women who'll know there's no woman to chase them around."

So I advertised, and found, amid ninety-five replies, Mrs. Bean, a paragon who loved finding dust and shifting it.

But we must return to the fireplace in the dusty room. What was Louis doing upstairs? The question was answered a minute later when he appeared clad only in a bathing costume.

"I think now I can get up the chimney," he said, hopefully, and proceeded to wriggle his way up. In a minute or so I could see nothing but a pair of muscular bare legs.

"Pass me some bricks, and some cement," said a voice from within.

This was not easy. Louis had entered with his arms above his head. Now he could not get them down. I managed to pass up a brick, and some dripping cement. Painfully, the sealing-up progressed. It was almost a mediæval scene, this walling up of a human body. Presently there was a howl of pain.

"The damn candle drops 'ot wax on my back," explained Louis.

But at last the job was finished. There were more anxious moments, when Louis looked like being a prisoner. He extricated himself finally, a strange piebald figure, bespattered with soot, candlewax and cement.

We cleaned up the mess, fixed the grate, laid a fire and then went off to have a bath. The lighting of the fire ⸻ ⸻ fireplace was to be a solemn ritual just be⸻ ⸻ When we descended again with shining ⸻ one would have recognised the grimy ⸻ the grimy bricklayer's labourer of half

⸻ ⸻ ⸻ of trial arrived. I applied a match to ⸻ Would it burn? There were anxious minutes. Fire lighting is always like a pro- pitiation of the ancient gods: they may refuse your sacrifice. One small flame began to feel at home. The good will spread. In five minutes there was a splendid crackling fire.

How jolly it looked! I had unearthed from the out- house an old basket grate. It had been discarded long ago, and lay rusty and broken. The back was separate from the front, it lacked a bottom. I removed from the back plate several layers of fire-corroded iron and discovered a delightful Adam-like design, an urn with floral streamers and two Cupids, with well-roasted posteriors, since they had sat over the hottest place. Four strips of iron off an old garden seat, neatly wired, made an admirable grating for the bottom, and when the whole thing had been given a coat of Brunswick black it looked most elegant.

The fire was now roaring away. Somehow the

character of the room was completely changed. It was more friendly, more cosy. That great cavernous fireplace had disappeared, and with it the draught. In the glow from the fire we surveyed our handiwork. A professional builder would have found obvious flaws—one did later, we had not 'tied' our bricks, nor overlapped the tiers in the prescribed professional manner—but what matter, it was our very own and pleasant to look upon.

I told Louis to open the bottle of Château-Laffitte. We should, of course, have christened the fireplace by breaking a bottle of champagne over it, but this would have made a fearful sizzle and mess, and I dislike seeing champagne wasted in this manner. Who started that idiotic mode of launching a ship?

While Louis tackled the bottle I opened a bag of chestnuts. There is a curious brass object hanging by my fireplace. It has a long handle and a round pan covered by a lid with holes in it. I had found it in a village antique shop. No one seemed to know what it was, and, a little doubtfully, general opinion had decided that it was a warming-pan for a baby's bed. Then one day a friend, wise in the history of the English home, saw it and laughed in derision at my description. "Nonsense! It's a chestnut roaster!" she said. And so it was.

I filled the roaster with chestnuts and put it on the fire. When they were roasted, pervading the room with a delicious aroma, Louis filled the glasses. We piled cushions on the floor and, squatting on them, drank to our fireplace and munched the hot chestnuts.

The flames leapt, the ruddy glow enveloped us and

Our Fireplace, from South Room

played between the dark beams of the ceiling, on the old pictures, bright silver and polished furniture. Never had the old room looked lovelier.

II

Strange, but the next morning there seemed something wrong with the fireplace. I said nothing to Louis about it, but quietly went on with my work. Turning suddenly, I caught him staring at the fireplace. Our eyes met.

"Well?" I asked.

"Don't you think it looks a little—a little——" began Louis.

"Funny—and not antique, I do," I answered.

"What is it?" he asked.

I did not answer at once, but stared at the fireplace. It looked a little gaunt and severe inside the old fireplace. On each side, from the mantelpiece to the hearth, there was a long deep gap, which I had intended for logs. They were depressing gaps.

"Wouldn't it be better if we filled them in?" asked Louis.

But I disliked wasting all that space. In a small cottage all space is precious. Suddenly I had an inspiration.

"I'm going to make two bookshelves," I said.

"Bookshelves? Where?"

"I'm going to divide those two gaps with a shelf each, and on the upper shelf we can put books, old books with faded leather bindings. They'll warm up the appearance of the chimney."

So we built a brick shelf, connecting each side of our new fireplace with the old. This finished, I selected my largest and oldest books. They nestled at once into their places and looked most homely. There was an antique and friendly air about the fireplace. What I did not foresee was that everyone who looked at our fireplace would ask the same question. "Doesn't it ruin the books?"

No, it doesn't ruin the books. The chimney never gets hot enough to heat the books, especially as they have thick leather covers. Moreover, it is an hospital for sickly books. Whenever I notice a book suffering from damp, with pains in its back, I put it on the fireplace shelf. After a week there all signs of rheumatism have disappeared.

FIRELIGHT

Now it is evening: draw the curtains close,
    The mist creeps round us from the grey hillside;
Here, in the firelight, let us think of those
    friends most with us in this eventide.

    t evening, in the camp fire's glow,
    r green fields seen from the cottage door,
    h for all the country sights they know—
    Autumn's beech leaves strew the valley's floor,

How the last apple on the topmost bough
    Glistens and reddens in the westering sun,
And hungry birds follow the heavy plough,
    And every chimney smokes with fires begun?

The hill that rises to the cloud-dark sky
    Is dearer still beneath the tropic blaze,
The lane that turns, the copse where rabbits lie
    Prick-eared in quick alarm, the frosty days

When the gay Hunt is up, on the lone veldt
    Grow lovelier in the exile's constant dream;
Oh England! where the wintry woods now melt
    In misty folds touched by the evening gleam!

Pile on the logs, among the rafters dark
    Send dancing shadows: here at England's core,
We'll keep a welcome warm till they embark
    And knock with eager hands upon the door.

CHAPTER XI

THE QUITE NAKED TRUTH

I

THE fireplace was neither the beginning nor the end of our labours. In the first year we had also made a rock garden, whitewashed the whole of the cottage outside, fitted bookshelves in the bedrooms and laid a new garden path. The path exhausted our bodies and tempers. I learnt that you buy gravel, not by weight, but by the square yard, and that a wheelbarrowful is as much as the strongest navvy can move. I had to move twenty wheelbarrowfuls only to learn that there is gravel and gravel. Mine was the second kind. It would not harden. Your feet sank into it. The garden roller went over it like a rolling-pin over dough with clay oozing at the edges. Finally, it all had to be dug up again, two days' hard labour, and mixed with concrete to give it body. All this had to be laid again and rolled. Then it rained and reduced it all to mud. The tradesmen finding their boots, as they dried, setting in concrete, threatened to boycott us.

To colour the path we had mixed Venetian red ochre with the gravel. Lady T., the very bright young wife of an old brewer baronet, must, of course, choose that day to call. She brought with her the most odious dog I have ever seen. It was a Pekinese, but as it suffered from hysteria which affected its coat, you never knew whether it would appear completely bald, like a wet rat, or fluffy-coated like a gosling. It was stone deaf, blind in one eye, and had no teeth. It required the complete attention of a junior chauffeur who carried a coat, a cushion, and a bottle of bromide pills for hysterical attacks. Lady T. also suffered from hysteria whenever she talked of 'the wicked dole.' That dog almost made me a Communist.

It was with certain malice that I saw Lady T. open my garden gate and delicately pick her way down the wet path. That dreadful dog followed, less cautiously. By the time it reached the door it was the subject for uncontrollable mirth, for it had plastered its stomach and encased its legs in red ochre. Lady T. had just crossed the threshold when she caught sight of her transformed dog. The alarm was raised at once. My servant was despatched for water, hot water not too hot, and a towel. An avalanche of endearments, protests, assurances were poured over that dog while it whimpered, rolled its one eye, and bared its toothless gums. There was a shriek when the wretched dog began to lick the red ochre off its paws and legs, staining its mouth.

"Darling! Darling, don't! Zu-mumsy-wumsy-oozy-noozy—no! Lambsy-woo-woo, don't, my darling," cried Lady T., pressing the animal to her breast.

"I don't think there's any arsenic in it," I said quietly.

Lady T.'s back arched in a way that suggested she had swallowed some.

"Oh, how terrible! How terrible! Such things shouldn't be used!" she cried.

The water and towel arrived. The dog was immersed. The coloured water looked like a blood-bath. After half an hour the commotion died down, and the miserable dog, swathed in a towel, shivered in Lady T.'s lap.

She never came again with that dog. She never came again herself. I am afraid I am regarded as a horrid man, unkind to animals.

II

I do not know how the idea of the sun-bathing platform emerged. I was an ardent sun-bather long before the medical profession made a cult of the thing they had so long opposed. In vain they were told of Dr. Rollier's marvellous cures in his chalets at Leysin, where nude brown bodies absorbed the healing light of the sun. Later, sun-bathing was to become a cult that turned every English seaside resort into a chilly Lido. Stockbrokers tanned their tummies with sun-ray lamps, and in Germany clothes became as scarce as a sense of humour.

The cult of nudism that swept over Germany was easily explicable. In a country so much at the mercy of the herd instinct, the opportunity of being absolutely alike was irresistible. Jack, if not as good as John, is the same as John with all his clothes off. A crowd of totally naked men, women and children, as I saw them in a compound near Lübeck, suffered from no social distinctions. A pair of young athletes, clothed only in a coat of tan, whom I invited to join me in a motor excursion to Lübeck, gave me a shock when I met them again, clothed, in the hall of the *naktkultur* club.   The velveteen jacket and shovel hat proclaimed one to be a Hamburg carpenter, the clothes of the other revealed the University student.   Nakedness is perhaps the surest basis of Socialism.   Perhaps the same instinct that moved large bodies of Germans to walk about with nothing on moved them to walk about in brown shirts and leggings, with their arms upraised.

My own sun-bathing owes nothing to politics or the herd instinct.   Happy months in Italy, Florida and North Africa have taught me the healing properties of sunlight judiciously absorbed.   It is a sad fact that almost one-third of the energy of the people in the British Isles is expended in keeping warm with adequate fires and clothing.   The Mediterranean countries are spared this effort.   We do not get enough sunlight, and the habit of heavily clothing ourselves through so many months of the year endures through those short intervals when our skin might achieve pigmentation and the blood effect a beneficial metabolism.

It is almost impossible for the town dweller to discard his clothing.   The practice of nakedness will bring his neighbours to the window with a pair of field-glasses, if not the police to the door.   The Recorder of London, shedding enlightenment on a dark Court, has exhorted the police to a crusade against exposure of the body, as made in the image of its Maker, what time clothed and armed burglars successfully evade the deluded and de-nuding police.   Happily a man's bath-room or garden is still his castle, if no one can see into it.

Unhappily my garden is overlooked in places.   A

broad-minded doctor, who allows his children to play like Cupids on the lawn, commands one angle, and an old cottage commands another.

I have said that Hans Andersen might well have lived in my cottage, instead of his dreary birthplace in Odense. He could also have found scene, plot and characters in the cottage beyond my garden. It is a tumbledown place, with crazy roof and chimney-pots awry, in which live two old bachelor brothers. They are woodcutters, who bring trunks from the beech-woods around, and deliver the hand-sawn logs with a pony as decrepit as themselves. Their cottage is in the middle of a lost garden, and the path to the front door has long been overgrown with wild brier.

Two sides of my garden being overlooked there is, fortunately, the south side. It faces an amphitheatre of hills crowned with glorious beechwoods. On this south side stands the garage, and at the side of the garage, between my four poplars and its roof, there is a space. It was here, level with the roof, overlooking the adjacent 'Roman road' and the amphitheatre, that I decided to build a sun-bathing platform. Thus placed, it raised me from observation either from my house or garden, and gave me, unseen, a commanding view of all approaches, and a glorious panorama of the valley and the high woods.

Nothing I have ever planned has given me more pleasure than this retreat. It cost exactly three pounds to build, and took us one week. We laid brick founda-tions for the four wooden pillars. The main frame was carefully mortised and tenoned with one side firmly clamped to the garage wall. The platform, at a height of twelve feet, was then surrounded by four sides, eighteen inches high, sufficient to protect us from observation while lying down, yet not obstructive to the view.   It was made large enough to accommodate six persons, which it was often called upon to do.   The most difficult piece of carpentry, Louis' *chef-d'œuvre*, and his legacy on leaving Pilgrim Cottage to perform his *Service Militaire* and resume life as a native of France, was the staircase.   It called for the most exact measurements and careful angles.   But it was triumphantly accomplished.

Naturally this mysterious erection created endless gossip in the village.   It became a favourite Sunday excursion for the inhabitants to saunter down the road and observe the 'goings-on.'   Nothing could be seen. For some time there was a general belief that it was a water-tank.   This changed to a swimming-pool, for an odd body in swimming costume had been descried. Then at last the truth was out.   *People were lying naked up there!*

From the very beginning of my advent into the village I had cultivated a reputation for eccentricity, since nothing affords so much freedom as this.   But my latest escapade was too much for the village mind, which surpasses any other in its relish of the scandalous. People were lying naked up there!   Gossip, penetrating viâ the kitchen, spoke of orgies behind my barricaded platform.   I carried on unperturbed.   Curiosity has a short life.   They saw figures ascending and descending in dressing-gowns.   Gradually they lost interest and I began to mow my lawn in slips.   No one looked through the holes in the hedge.   Tanned torsos

and legs called for no more comment than cabbages.
The neighbouring doctor aided and abetted. We could
have founded a *naktkultur* colony.

III

The platform was a success from the start. Facing
south, and sheltered from the winds, there were days
when it was even too hot and I had to descend. But
there were weeks when I lay there in almost Mediterranean warmth, gazing up at the poplars slightly swaying in the blue sky. It was a revelation of how much
it is possible to sun-bathe in the English climate. I had
always been derisive about English sunshine, accustomed as I was to Italy, but I discovered to my surprise
that there were days in April and days in October when
the sun was warm enough to discard all clothing.

How many happy days, permeated by the warmth of
the sun, I have spent on that platform, lying on my mat-
tress, dreaming or reading, turning now this way, now
that, to achieve the sun-bather's glory—a thorough and
even tan. There is such a thing as sun intoxication, so
different from sunstroke. One just wishes to lie there
hour after hour, worries gone, ambitions dormant, all
the cares of life dissolved in blissful content.

There were hours when I worked there also. Three-
quarters of this book were written in the blaze of the
sun, when I wore nothing but a white hat and a pair of
sun-glasses, my back resting on piled-up cushions,
while I wrote in a manuscript book curling with the
heat. At week-ends there were sun parties, with
cigarettes, lemonade, laughter and a necessary supply

of olive-oil for sore skins.   Nature in nothing serves us
equally.   She gives some of us skins that pigment,
some of us skins that blister; to a few the sun is
poison.

The sun-bather has his own form of vanity.   I had
observed on the Lido how much an habitué was
annoyed by the swifter and deeper pigmentation of a
newcomer.   I myself laboriously acquiring a 'coat'
after a month of exposure, had been moved to jealousy
by a five-day achievement of some lucky sun-bather.
Dark-complexioned people always soar ahead of the
fair, and the possessor of freckles is generally a painful
peeler.

There were advantages and disadvantages from the
position of the platform.   I had command of the road
before my gate.   I could survey visitors from over my
parapet while they were quite unaware of my proximity.
I could also hear conversations in the road, often concerning my cottage, my garden and myself.   I heard
two shy autograph hunters discuss whether I was ap-
proachable or disagreeable.   They were young ladies
with Kodak cameras and albums and emerged from a
small car.   One cautious look told me they would not
find me disagreeable, except in the matter of being
'snapped.'   In the best attire I am grossly libelled by
the camera.   My face was never photographable, and
the finest camera piles misfortune on misfortune.   In
these days when authors are much seen a good profile
seems better than a good style.

Sometimes in the heat of the day I have fallen
asleep.   One disadvantage of my retreat is that I cannot get into the house without being seen by visitors.

There was an occasion, during a discussion of a scenario of a book of mine, when it seemed as if the whole staff of the Gaumont-Gainsborough had descended upon me. I had been asleep, so had not heard the large car in which the scenario writer, a lady assistant, a casting director, another assistant, etc., had arrived at my gate. My housekeeper, a little bewildered, showed them to seats on the lawn, and while they were engaged in conversation, I flitted by, clad in a bright beach-gown and a large sun-hat. One of the visitors caught a glimpse of me, then looked rapidly away. They stayed to lunch, and a chance remark made me aware that they expected to meet my wife (?)—the lady glimpsed in the bathgown and hat!

There was an occasion, too, on a gloriously hot July day, when, my servant being out, I had to descend, scantily clad, to attend to a young man vigorously knocking at my door. He tried to hide his surprise when someone looking like a native of the South Seas accosted him. He introduced himself as representing a firm of valuers. He had heard I possessed some valuable pictures. Surely it would be wise to insure them. He cast an eye over my cottage. It was the kind of place that would burn quickly, he hinted, unkindly. The pictures would be a serious loss.

"On the contrary, I'd be glad to lose them," I replied.

Again I saw a quick suspicion that I was a lunatic.

"They're too big for the cottage, and they're not mine."

"Not yours?"

"They belong to my family, they're heirlooms. I

am obliged to store them, but I can't see why I should pay an insurance tax on them, for the ultimate benefit of someone who may be equally embarrassed by them."

This seemed a new attitude towards ancestors. But he recovered and began an eloquent argument.

I observed him closely. He was a pleasant young fellow of about twenty-two, but there was something incongruous in his appearance in my garden this hot July afternoon. He was so typical, so faultlessly 'produced,' a piece of Bond Street in a corner of the Chilterns. He wore a stiff white collar, a bowler hat, and a tight-fitting black coat and vest, with pin-stripe trousers. There was not a flaw from the crown of his Scott hat to the sole of his patent shoes. The pearl pin was the right size, the gold watch-chain of the right slimness. He wore the inevitable crested signet ring on the little finger of his left hand. Every inch of him proclaimed Public School, the doctrine of football and fortitude. He was so correct, so eager, so naïve.

"Tell me," I said cruelly, "you have a Brigg umbrella?"

"Why, yes—but not here," he replied, surprised.

"And a bed-sitting-room in the West End?"

"Yes," he said, his eyes widening.

"And, possibly, you were born in a vicarage?"

"Good heavens! How do you know all that, sir!" he cried, shaken out of his self-possession.

I smiled at him. He was a likeable youth.

"I happen to be a novelist. Like detectives, we practise observation and deduction," I said. "You're hot, I see."

He had removed his bowler-hat, leaving a red line

on his smooth brow, and with a handkerchief wiped away the perspiration.

"Wouldn't you like to get rid of all those things?" I asked, tantalisingly.

"Gosh! Wouldn't I!" he exclaimed. "What a gloriout spot this is, sir!"

"Then do," I said. "Come in, I'll find you a costume."

He laughed, hesitated, laughed again.

"Well, that's an idea, sir. May I?"

Half an hour later, as he lay on the cushions on the platform, and watched the cigarette smoke ascend in the still air, he said—

"Jove! this is perfect. Only one thing worries me."

"What's that?"

"I really ought to be working—I was sent down to get insurances."

"Well, you've got one."

He raised his head from the cushions and looked at me.

"How, sir?"

"Since you know how to appreciate the cottage, you shall have the insurance of it."

"Oh, thanks, sir. What a perfect afternoon!"

Before we descended for tea in the shade of an apple tree, I had found that all my surmises were correct. He was born in a vicarage, educated at Marlborough, had a bed-sitting-room in South Kensington, and had bought his hat at Scott's, and his umbrella at Brigg's. When he knew me a little better he called me 'a wizard fellow,' which I took as a compliment.

Tilly 'bathed' twice on the platform. On the second occasion she brought a friend, a Javanese actress whose petite face and coffee-coloured skin gave an exotic air to my garden. I expected to hear temple bells burst forth, my thrushes sing like bulbuls, and the poplars bloom with pomegranate flowers. The butcher's boy, a lusty youth, calling for orders, nearly fainted when he saw her crossing the garden, wrapped in a white towel, with almond eyes, brown legs and pink toe-nails. He forgot to give Beau Brummell, my cocker spaniel, his usual bone, and his whole nervous system must have been deranged, for he seemed incapable of starting up his delivery van outside my gate.

I do not think Tilly really enjoyed sun-bathing. She insisted that her head, neck, arms, hands and knees should not be exposed. She wore a white farm-wife's bonnet that completely buried her. Then she put on cotton gloves to save her hands, covered her knees with a towel, and declared she adored sun-bathing. She had brought with her a portable gramophone and half a dozen terrible records she had discovered in Paris. She assured me they were by a new French *diseuse* who was an absolute genius. When I heard them I said I thought a new French disease would be a better description, whereupon Tilly revenged herself by telling me she had just been examining my apple trees and had discovered they had been attacked by the American blight.

"You mean they're taking to jazz?" I asked scoffingly.

"Don't be silly. It's very serious. It's woolly aphis. If you don't believe me go and see. You'll find something that looks like cotton-wool on the boughs. Squeeze some of it between your fingers, it's gummy, and you'll crush a red insect inside."

I went down to the apple trees. Strange, but I had never noticed these bits of cotton-wool sticking all over the boughs. I took some between my fingers and squeezed it. As I had been told, it was gummy and was stained with the red blood of an insect. I looked at the filthy mess in dismay. It was all over the tree, in little pockets of bark.

"What does it do to the tree?" I asked Tilly. "Will it ruin my crop?"

"Of course it will. You'll have to spray the tree this winter, and disinfect the ground, and burn every leaf that falls, and——"

"Good heavens!" I cried. "It sounds like the small-pox!"

"It is the smallpox."

"I believe you're merely trying to depress me, just because I've caught you with a French disease."

"Very well," said Tilly, ominously. "You wait and see."

"The statesman who first said that became very unpopular," I retorted, weakly.

I was very upset, and spent several hours the next day making enquiries. It was all hideously true.

I swear that when I mentioned my trouble to a gardening neighbour, who, having retired from business, has sentenced himself to life slavery in his garden, his face lit up with horrid joy.

"Well, now," he said, "it's a funny thing I was only reading this morning—now where is it—in—in—now what was it in——"

Here he began to turn over a collection of papers and magazines that made his den look like a hairdresser's salon.

"Ah, here it is—now read that!" he said, thrusting a gardening weekly into my hands. "And when you've read it, just forget it all. If you start waging war on every pest in your garden, you'll never have a minute's peace. Nations survive wars and gardens survive pests. Come along and have a look at my celery."

But I found it hard to be enthusiastic over his bumptiously healthy celery. I diligently read the paper he gave me, and grew more depressed.

One result of our glorious summer's sunshine has been a great plague of American blight or woolly aphis on apple trees. The warm conditions have just been such that this very troublesome and destructive pest has flourished and multiplied at a prodigious rate. . . .

So while I was rejoicing in the sunshine on my platform, happy in the glorious heat, the aphis, equally happy, had been multiplying. I read on about the reckless aphis:

In our own garden, despite incessant warfare against it, one or two trees get fresh infestations annually, because over the garden wall are some old trees that are left to harbour all the pests they can hold and their surplus population seek and reach our trees.

This began to sound like Signor Mussolini awarding the triplets prize and acclaiming a more potent Empire, or Japan explaining her presence in Manchuria. I read on:

We have considerably reduced the numbers of these unwanted visitors by summer pruning young shoots, and consigning them with their wool-clad tenants——

Wool-clad tenants!—this sounded rather like garden hosiery, and altogether too friendly towards the little beasts—

—immediately to the incinerator. For the rest we are waiting for their descent to the roots of the trees, where they take up winter quarters, and then soil fumigants will be used to choke them to death.

Ah! choke them to death. I liked that remorseless note. But this fumigating business suggested an isolation hospital rather than a garden. I thought of my neighbour's light indifference. Was he the infecting source? Why did not the Government deal drastically with such slackness? They were firm about Foot and Mouth Disease, as every church-door showed.

My eye caught another paragraph on the open page. A fascination of horror made me read on.

Scab diseases and other leaf troubles have been rife in many gardens this year, and it will do much to check their reappearance if the diseased leaves are raked off the ground and gathered up for burning with as little delay as possible. The spore-filled pustules on these do not rot when the tissues of the leaves decompose; they simply wait in the soil until——

The spore-filled pustules . . . wait until. A shiver went down my spine. I looked out into the sunlit garden, but it had become a battlefield of horror. I remembered the dismay that filled me one morning when I found some of the young lupins had drooped their heads, heavy with promise of bloom. When I examined them I discovered that filthy slugs had almost eaten through their stems. A little soot sprinkled on the plants had stopped further massacre. But now I knew there was a menace underground as well as above. Every falling leaf was a menace. For the first time I felt the dismay and terror of Shelley's *Sensitive Plant*, a Dantean vision of an horticultural Hell.

> *And agarics and fungi, with mildew and mould*
> *Started like a mist from the wet ground cold;*
> *Pale, fleshy, as if the decaying dead*
> *With a spirit of growth had been animated!*

Well, something had to be done. I would never succumb to my neighbour's laissez-faire. Tilly was right, as ever. It was a kind of smallpox.

It had never occurred to me that there were such things as soil fumigants. With Browning I had been inclined to shout "Oh, the smile of the good brown earth!" That it could grin or leer was a shock.

Turning over the gardening weekly I was astonished by an advertisement that told me I could sterilise the soil electrically. "By means of electrical heating the steriliser treats every particle of soil, killing the harmful bacteria." I was reminded at once of the electric scalp massage I had been offered so frequently in vain. Electric heating for houses is now widespread, but electric heating for garden soil suggests frightful quarterly bills.

In an adjacent column I was offered a special rake to deal with the noxious spore-filled pustules that refused to decay:

> Only the sluggish gardener leaves these leaves (a trained author wanted here) as harbourage for slugs and other pests . . . and if your lawn is mossy nothing is so good as our rake for making moss mizzle.

Ah, I would buy one and make the moss mizzle!

There are women who trade in reminiscences of sickness. They are only happy when narrating their battles with terrible afflictions. I began to be afflicted this way in regard to my garden, and quickly found other gardeners with frightful symptoms. Dining one evening with a friend who keeps six gardeners, I brought up the subject of woolly aphis. He seemed delighted and sent at once for his head gardener.

"Smith'll tell you all about. He's wonderful! He knows all the ailments of plants."

Smith duly arrived, was shown into the study, asked to sit down, and given a glass of port. He expanded at once, but I did not learn anything to give me comfort. It transpired that American blight was a kind of rheumatism. It got into the tree and made its joints all knotty.

"It gnarls them something awful, sir."

"But what do you do about it?"

"You paint the tree."

"Paint it—with a brush?"

"Yessir. All over with paraffin or methylated spirit."

"But it's impossible! Mine's a big tree. It would take a week, and then I'd miss parts of it. Can you fumigate the soil—don't the insects go down into it during the winter?"

"Never heard o' that, sir," said Smith, shaking his head.

"And if I don't paint the tree—what happens?"

"You'll have no fruit. You'd better chop the tree down, if you can't paint it."

"But I'm told that if I burn the leaves and fumigate——"

"You've been reading them gardening papers, and them adverts. Don't believe 'em, sir," said Smith, finishing the port.

I was about to protest that I had never heard two gardeners who agreed about anything, but the port or the expression on my face encouraged him to further disclosures. He gave us a long discourse on the frightful things that menace everything in the garden. He did not stop there; he went on into the greenhouse, and began to tell me all about the mealy bugs that attack the vines. I tried to bring him back to the woolly aphis, but his heart was set on mealy bugs.

"Shall we go and play squash?" I said, desperately, to my host, feeling I could bear it no longer. Grimly I decided I would not paint my trees, I would not cut them down. I had a feeling that apple trees had flourished long before gardeners painted them with paraffin or methylated spirits. Eve had been given an apple, Venus had been given an apple, despite the woolly aphis.

But I decided to buy a soil fumigant as a lazy way out. The morning it arrived I read in *The Times* that England's lovely elm trees were being attacked by a mysterious disease that threatened the beauty of our countryside; that Cuba was in the throes of a revolution; that Germany had walked out of the League of Nations, and that there was considerable uneasiness concerning the appearance in several districts of the antirrhinum disease, which for many years had been a serious trouble in America.

This was altogether too much for me. I could suffer Cuba to have a revolution, Germany to burn its Reichstag and click its heels, but the thought of another American blight attacking my beloved antirrhinums was altogether too much. I felt I should be happier in a flat than in a poisoned paradise where everything seemed doomed.

SUNSTRUCK

It is good to lie in the sun and forget
The things to be done, the ills that fret
The heart of man, whose ambitious ways
Rob him of joy in these summer days.
For I count him truly wealthy who
Can dream all day, with nothing to do
But watch the old mare on the fence
Scratch her mane; or make pretence
That butterflies in noonday hours
Are disembodied souls of flow'rs.

The noonday hums with busy bees
But more industrious than these
The lark, with ceaseless effort, soars
To cast his song at Heaven's doors
In scorn of idiot-cuckoos, low
On earth, who only two notes know!
And my four poplars will not bend
Their heads, nor even condescend
To throw their shadows on the ground,
Where two old cows, in a profound
And tranquil meditation, keep
Aloof from woolly-headed sheep!

CHAPTER XII

THE MISERABLE WORM

HAVING written about pests, let us turn to the miserable worm. Let me introduce my friend Lumbricus, who does more work in the garden than any of us. He is much maligned, he has always been treated with contempt, dug up and flung aside for birds to gobble, or chopped up by callous small boys. Lumbricus is, of course, the lowly worm. But he is lowly only in our ignorant minds. We use him as a simile in a moment of utter contempt or protest. "What a worm that man is!" or "Even a worm will turn," we exclaim.

Now if we only knew, there could be no higher compliment than to call a man a worm, for a worm is, probably, the most important animal, Man excepted, in all Creation. He has changed the whole face of Nature; he has truly turned the world upside down.

I should not have developed an admiration for my friend Lumbricus had I not been irritated by his autumn habits. If you do not sweep up the leaves on your lawn as soon as they fall, then the worm will add considerably to your labours. He delights in pulling leaves into the ground, so firmly that the besom will not dislodge them, and you must go down on your hands and knees and pull out each leaf.

It was this troublesome habit that set me thinking about worms, and started me upon astonishing discoveries. It is singular that the most important thing in the garden remains comparatively unknown to the gardener. I have pursued my enquiries among the most intelligent professional gardeners and their ignorance is abysmal. They have a slightly hostile attitude to Lumbricus, and if not hostile they are contemptuous.

I have asserted that worms change the face of Nature. This is a fact, not a generalisation. On each acre of land some eighteen tons of earth annually pass through their bodies and are brought to the surface. This means that the superficial bed of mould, which we commonly call the soil, passes through their bodies every few years. They are the real ploughers of the land. Collapsing burrows, the manufacture of humus acids in their intestines by the digestion of half-decayed leaves, the small stones that pass through their gizzards and suffer disintegration by powerful muscular action, all these things enrich and change the soil.

Lumbricus not only renews the soil, keeping it aerated with his burrows, thus exposing fresh surfaces to the action of the carbonic acid in the soil, he changes the external face of Nature. He is a great leveller, he is the true Socialist of the soil. The castings we see on the lawn in the morning, to our great annoyance, are evidence of the worm's passion for levelling. Every year he brings to the surface a layer of earth, in the form of castings, a quarter of an inch thick. These castings are washed down by rain, or having dried, are blown about. On an incline a considerable body of earth is therefore moved down to the valley, over a period of time almost negligible in the consideration of a geologist.

Charles Darwin, who was never satisfied with what only his eyes showed him, made a study of the lowly Lumbricus. Amazing to relate, he wrote a book on worms that was a best-seller in its time! It sold ten thousand copies, a number that fills even successful novelists with envy. *Vegetable Mould and Earth-Worms* he called his book. I found it as exciting as any detective thriller, and it was much more real, for Charles Darwin tracked down every elusive speculation to the scientific facts. He never let any idea escape him, or run loose.

The worm is not only the gardener's friend, he is the archæologist's friend, and the sworn enemy of the jerry builder. Many objects not liable to decay are, in the course of time, buried under the castings of worms and thus preserved. Much of Roman Britain, its villas and tessellated pavements, has been saved for us by those small curators. The burrow of the worm rarely goes deeper than five feet. It follows that buildings with sound foundations, deeper than five feet, are safe from undermining and subsidence of the soil by the worm's activities. Thus the solid monuments are immune from attack. It is jerry building that is menaced by the worm.

For this and other reasons Darwin's admiration was aroused by our friend Lumbricus—

When we behold a wide, turf-covered expanse, we should remember that its smoothness, on which so much of its beauty depends, is mainly due to all the inequalities having been slowly levelled by worms. . . . The plough is one of the more ancient and valuable of man's inventions, but long before it existed the land was in fact regularly ploughed by earthworms. It may be doubted whether there are many other animals which have played so important a part in the history of the world, as have these lowly organised creatures.

Darwin told me much, but I had my own investigations to make. Certain facts I had established by observation, others were proven by experimentation. Worms, for instance, can move in either direction, though they have heads and tails. A worm chopped in two or three pieces joins up again with itself. The ends overlap and are bound round with a new skin, much as a broken stick is bound together, and not as the carriages of a train are coupled. A chopped worm, therefore, after re-union, is shorter than its former self. It is a clumsy surgeon in the eyes of the Royal College of Surgeons.

Worms have no eyes, but they can distinguish slowly day from night. They are nocturnal in their habits, but not venturesome. They crawl about, with their tails still inserted in their burrows. They never quite leave home. They hate dry air, which is fatal to them yet, strange to say, they dislike damp air, and they plug the entrance to their burrows with fallen leaves to keep out the cold. In the heat of summer, and in winter when the ground is frozen, they dig to a considerable depth and then cease work until climatic conditions improve.

Like most children, I was told when very young that the early bird catches the worm. "Why?" I demanded, to the annoyance of my elders, to whom the moral of rising early and being rewarded seemed obvious. "But if the worm wasn't there the bird wouldn't get it, no matter how early it got up!" I said, and was dismissed as an idiot. My infant mind wanted to know why the worm was out. Did it get up early, if so, how disastrous was early rising for the worm! Did it stay out all night?—there might be a moral in this. But my elders seemed both ignorant and impatient. "The early bird catches the worm," they repeated, like parrots.

Why, if the bird is early enough, does he catch the worm? Before answering this conundrum of my infancy let me say that often the bird only catches a part of the worm. Lumbricus has a prodigious power of latitudinal as well as longitudinal expansion. I have said that he keeps his tail in the burrow while taking an airing. By expansion of his tail and with the help of the reflexed bristles on his body he can hold so fast that he cannot be dragged out of the ground by a bird, and rather than let go he will suffer himself to be torn into pieces.

Since worms have no eyes they cannot see light, yet they are sensible to light, but only from its duration and intensity. It is probable that the light passes through their skins, and, exciting their cerebral ganglia, makes them conscious of it. Now this is a slow process, and one may presume that a worm out at night is often unconscious of the first approach of dawn, and this gives the early bird its chance.

I state this, after experimentation with lights, as a probability. There is also the fact that worms like lying near the surface of their burrows in order to enjoy breathing the fresh air. Those who remain throughout the night in their plugged burrows get what the Navy calls 'a good fug' on, and with the rising temperature, after dawn, they come out for a breather. A close observer can see them in their burrows with their heads just slightly withdrawn.

The leaves that I found pulled down into the burrows served several purposes. They were for food, for lining the upper parts of the burrows, but mostly for plugging the hole to keep out the damp cold. They generally seize the top of a broad leaf and pull it in a depth of an inch or a half, with the result that the leaf is crumpled up and makes a satisfactory plug. Occasionally the stalk is seized, but the tip of the leaf is more popular. I noticed that they rather like the long stalks of chestnut leaves, something like miniature thigh-bones, and some of these I found pulled in to a depth of two inches.

The worm has a mouth and no nose, but he breathes through his skin. The nervous system that serves as a brain runs the whole length of the body, hence his ability to join up with separated parts. He can travel either way, he has a sense of smell and is completely deaf. But he has a sense of touch and is very sensitive to vibrations. Has he a sense we know little of? I still wonder, and the reason is this.

It was my habit to place the worms I dug up on my bird-table, some three feet from the ground. I noticed that these worms would always crawl to the edge, and stretch out their anterior ends into space, seeking a place to journey to.   After much investigation of space they always fell on to the garden bed below. I noticed, however, that the fall was intentional, not accidental.   After stretching out very cautiously and never losing balance, there came a moment when they deliberately hurled themselves into space.   A three feet fall into the unknown is a prodigious one for a worm. Was it deliberate suicide or mere recklessness?   Did they sense that earth was far below them?

I made an experiment.   Under the right end of the bird-table, on the garden bed, I placed a bucket of water.   I then put half a dozen worms on the platform and watched the result.   Every worm hurled itself into space off the three sides of the platform, not one chose the end over the bucket.   I repeated the experiment three times, with the same result.   I decided it was not suicide, but instinct.   The worms knew that earth was below except in one place.

They like cabbage leaves, onion and chopped meat. I used this knowledge in my experiments on worm-power.   I wanted to discover their muscular strength apart from their clinging ability proved by the remorse-less bird.   For this purpose I took a six-foot plank, with two edges half an inch high.   The trough thus made I filled with firm earth.   At the far end I placed a full flower-pot with cabbage leaves and chopped meat on the surface.   I then took three sturdy worms of equal size and attached an ounce, half-ounce, and quarter-ounce weight, respectively, to their tails by means of a piece of cotton.   I then put them all at the far end of my earth track and awaited results.   I had to repeat this experiment five times, for the worms were often bad starters. Some turned round and went the wrong way. Finally I halved the distance of the track. At last I got three 'runners.'

They had just sufficient earth with which to bury themselves and thus gain pulling power. In less than an hour the worm with the quarter-ounce handicap had disappeared in the flower-pot at the end of the track, and in two hours the half-ounce competitor had also, reached the pot. But the ounce worm had only succeeded in traversing half the length by the next morning, a period of twenty-four hours, and after two days, having proceeded three-quarters of the way, it gave up the struggle and lay dormant.

Repetitions produced several quarter- and half-ounce worms that reached the pot, but not one ounce starter succeeded. Three lay dormant, two succumbed, and four turned back or meandered about, as if discouraged. I assume, therefore, that a worm averaging three grammes can pull half to three-quarters of an ounce, but cannot pull an ounce. Measurement seemed to prove, somewhat roughly, that worm-power is in a ratio of three times its own weight, about twice that of a normal man.

With worms Nature demonstrates her relentless capacity for destruction as well as creation in a world that poor mortals persist in regarding as pacific. Man is a casual enemy whose gardening brings prodigious upheavals, but birds are voracious enemies capable of devouring one hundred feet of worm a day.

I do not know to what extent worms plug up their burrows with leaves as a defence work. I have been aware that there is often a strange urgency in this work, and friends have assured me that on calm evenings they have heard a rustling noise proceeding from worms seizing dry leaves and plugging their burrows. This plugging may arise from a desire to stop the ingress of the chill night air which they dislike, just as we try to stop the draught under a door, but it may also arise from a desire to conceal the burrows from a deadly enemy, the Scolopendra or centipede, or those ferocious beetles, the Staphylinus and Carabus, that attack by night when the burrows are opened.

The odds seem all against the worm, but their fecundity keeps pace with their defencelessness. As many as 55,000 have been estimated to exist in an acre of garden land, or about 360 pounds in weight, assuming an average weight of 3 grammes. But although a worm can turn it cannot attack, as the simile would suggest. They work hard, for half the year, laying off in dry weather or frosts, and their output of earth turned averages around eighteen tons per acre per year. They live in the superficial mould, and most of their casting, either by direct burrowing or the passing of soil through their bodies, is done at a depth preferably from four to ten inches.

Sexually they are hermaphroditic, that is, two sexes are united in the same individual, but two individuals pair together. Their love-affairs are complicated. They engage in a reciprocal act, but each simultaneously functions as both male and female. The two worms place themselves side by side, but head to tail, and their contact lasts for a considerable time. In the anterior third of their bodies there is a thickening, called the clitellum, which pours out a mucous secretion. This by degrees forms a band round the two worms and then hardens, fastening them firmly together.

The next stage begins in the fifteenth segment of each worm, where the male reproductive opening pours out its spermatophores. Intense muscular contraction carries these loose spermatophores along to the ninth and tenth segments, where the seminal pouches are located. Thus the pouches of the two worms are crowded with one another's spermatophores.

This would seem to be the end. Actually it is only a beginning and what follows seems incredible. They have not gone through this process to fertilise their own ova. The two worms go off and each finds a new partner, whose ova are fertilised by the semen of the old partners, who have acted merely as intermediaries!

Considered all in all, my sympathies are with the worms. They get little out of life save a few dead leaves, they are constantly preyed upon, chopped up, gobbled, frozen or pulled to pieces. They labour in the earth with astonishing industry and far-reaching results to the soil's productivity, and get little acknowledgment and no thanks.

When people wish to be contemptuous they call a man 'a worm.' When they wish to show pity to an ill-treated man they say he has 'a dog's life.' Yet in my observation the dog is a highly favoured creature, comfortably housed, well fed, fondled and safely kept. Should we not rather say of an unfortunate man that he has a worm's life? I think so.

THE ROMAN VILLA

How clever were those Roman fingers
  Working here,
Now only a little lingers
  From that far year,
When last this pavement sounded,
  Hadrian spoke,
The trireme galleys grounded,
  From this hearth rose smoke.

How little has the landscape altered,
  These uplands green
Where Claudius' cattle faltered;
  And there between
Those fallen gates, now crumbled,
  The chariot ran,
The Roman street once rumbled
  With the traffic of man.

How futile were the hopes they nourished,
  Foolish indeed,
For even as they flourished
  There grew Time's seed
To split their stones asunder,
  However firm,
While over and while under
  Worked the lowly worm.

CHAPTER XIII

CONCERNING PLINY AND PLOT

I

THE other day I was reading some letters of an old friend. He was fortunate in the possession of several estates. I never knew a man who had a deeper love of gardens and who lived the country life to higher perfection. He was an Italian with large business interests in Rome, but his heart was always in the country. He had settled in a villa of his own building within easy reach of the city. "It occupies an excellent position on the coast," he wrote, "and is near enough to Rome (seventeen miles to be exact) for me to be able to get back in the evening before dinner."

I never saw his villa, but he gave me the fullest description of it. It was the usual double-winged type, with a formal garden in the centre, always beautifully kept. The library was a feature of the villa, "a quiet spot which catches most of the sun and is so protected that you never hear the wind except when a storm brings up the clouds and drives us indoors. The library stands close by under a dome-shaped roof, with windows looking out in every direction. The walls are filled with shelves to hold my books—the kind of books which one not only reads but studies. Adjoining the library is a bedroom on either side of the passage, heated by hot-water pipes running under the floor."

His villa was architect-planned. The garden had a promenade running around it. "I have planted it with box hedges or with rosemary where box will not grow. I find the box grows excellently where it is protected by buildings. Within the promenade young vines are planted. These give a pleasant shade; you can walk under them even with bare feet. Mulberry and fig trees also do very well in this soil, and are as attractive to look at as the sea itself. Round at the back, towards the vestibule, lies the kitchen garden."

I think that kitchen garden was a concession to his uncle, a distinguished and stern old Admiral, who had also been his country's Ambassador in Spain. The uncle greatly deplored the luxurious habits of the younger generation, and he never ceased to preach the merits of the simple life. He even railed against flower gardens in Rome, and asserted that every citizen should have a vegetable plot, sufficient to feed himself, as in the good, simple old days. "Oh, what a blessed, what a harmless and secure life that was so long as men could be content with such a pittance and stay so!" he wrote in a book I have by me.

He must have regarded his nephew's villa with disapproval, but no censure escaped him. Poor old fellow, he came to a sad though noble end. As Admiral of the Fleet, he was sent to the coast off Pompeii when a terrible eruption overwhelmed Pompeii and Herculaneum. While gallantly attempting to rescue the inhabitants, he was suffocated by the fumes. For the uncle of whom I write was the Elder Pliny, a boy when Pontius Pilate ruled in Judæa, and a youth when London was founded by a Roman general.

He was a man of considerable culture and wrote a *Natural History*, much admired by our Elizabethans, and never out of the hands of the learned Dr. Plot, of whom more anon. Both the elder and younger Pliny were born at Como, that pleasant town at the foot of the Italian lake, which I often visit on my way out to Venice.

Besides his two villas on the sea coast, young Pliny had a delightful villa on Lake Como, where I was once the guest, nearly two thousand years later, of its present owner, the Marchese Torti. The garden by the lake possesses a remarkable spring that ebbs and flows every three hours in response to some subterranean force. When Shelley visited the place he was fascinated by this mysterious pool and wrote a description of it.

How vain we are to imagine that our experiences are unique! The same habits, the same thoughts, the same ambitions and anxieties seem to have dominated man through civilisations now lost in dust. Young Pliny, driving home to his villa after a day's work in the City, thinking of a contract he had just made, of the rose trees he intended to plant, or the opening he must find for his son, seems only to have exchanged a car for a chariot, a tail coat for a toga. In the morning he is sharp with the slave boy bringing round the horses: he is late for the City.

I amused myself building a sun platform. Young Pliny built a chalet in his grounds. "I am quite in love with it, for I built it myself," he writes. "It has a sunny room facing the walk on one side and the sea on the other, and an apartment with folding doors opening on to the cloisters with a window facing the sea."

He describes its enchanting views, and when I am apt to preen myself on installing steam heating in an English cottage I fall silent on thinking of Pliny in his 'chalet,' where he might have heard one morning that a man called Paul of Tarsus, belonging to a crazy sect of Christians, had been crucified in the City. "How stupid to make martyrs of these fellows!" he probably said to a neighbour. "It only helps to advertise them."

I have often thought of a garden annexe such as Pliny built for himself. You could lounge or work in it. "A delightfully quiet bedroom leads out of this room. It is entirely shut off from the voices of the slave boys, the murmur of the sea, the raging of the tempests or the flash of lightning, unless the windows are left open. Every sound is deadened by a passage running between the bedroom wall and the garden. The bedroom is heated by a small apparatus which you can turn off and on, as you wish, by shutting a small trap-door."

52 A.D., and the same system is still in use in many English and French houses! I often stay in a villa at Auteuil, fifteen minutes from the Arc de Triomphe, which has neat trap-doors in the floor through which comes the heating.

And Pliny liked old clothes, and to potter in his garden. "One can retire there and be less interrupted. It is so snug and comfortable. You need not put on your best toga. Nobody comes to call on you. . . . My household, too, are never in better health than here. So far (I touch wood) I have not lost a single servant."

No, there was no worry from touts at the door,

musicians in the streets, or the necessity, apparently, of having the cook well flogged.   All was peace.

I have an hospitable friend who in his park has built a covered tennis court and swimming pool.   It is rather like staying with the younger Pliny.   "A large cheerful dressing-room takes you to the swimming bath.   If you prefer a more bracing swim in the open a fish pond lies in the court."   Given a hot summer's day, Berkshire so easily becomes Tuscany, Lord Iliffe a noble Roman, and myself a scribe taking a respite from his stylus and wax tablets.

II

Reading Pliny's *Letters* to-day, one expects to find the telephone number and nearest station at the head of them, so typical are they of missives from a modern country house.

The Elder Pliny has never had a more enthusiastic reader than my learned friend, Dr. Robert Plot, whom I must now introduce.   I first met him by chance in the Charing Cross Road.   I was looking for some old, large, leather-bound tomes to put on the shelves I had made at the side of the fireplace.   Antiquity was more important than contents.   I wanted books that looked well-settled.   Presently my eye fell on a leatherback of this nature, and the title was an additional recommendation.   It was an octavo volume, in half calf, with tooled back, entitled *Natural History of Oxfordshire*. A glance at the contents showed that it was printed in 1677, 'at the Theater in Oxford,' dedicated 'To the Most Sacred Majesty of Charles the Second,' and written by R. P., LL.D.

Modest and most learned Dr. Plot!   He thus effaced himself on the title-page, and coyly emerged, low down on the right-hand corner of the last page of an eloquent preface ending

Your Majesties most Loial
and
most obedient
Subject,
Rob. Plot.

Words fail me in presenting Dr. Plot.   Truly, he was a man who knew everything.   He peered into every corner of Oxfordshire, almost into every house it would seem.   No legend was too wild, no gossip too slight, no investigation too laborious, no journey too tiresome, and no subject too obscure for his inquisitive mind.   Only once does he appear to have been repulsed.   I fear the farmers of Oxfordshire were rude to him.   He was enquiring into their soil and they do not seem to have liked it.

More possibly might have been added to this general account of *Earths*, and not a little instructive to the *Farmers* of the Country, but I found most of them froward and to slight my *Queries;* let them thank themselves if I am not so obliging.   Beside, it seems a business a little beside my *design*, therefore in haste I proceed to a more particular consideration of Earths. . . . But herein I shall not shew myself either so angry or ignorant, or so much either disrespect my subject, or the civilities of the *Gentry* for the sake of the *clowns*. . . .

Not exactly the retort courteous, but weightily done. Dr. Plot was not an Oxfordshire man. He was born in Kent. In middle life he was appointed the first keeper of the Ashmolean Museum, and to this appointment and his own ceaseless curiosity, mixed a little with a vanity for airing his scholarship, we owe this *Natural History*. It may have been suggested, too, by the veneration in which he held the *Natural History* of the Elder Pliny, with which he is always making comparisons.

Dr. Plot, on the whole, keeps very much in the background. He delights in paying lavish tributes to his learned friends, to 'the mellifluous Dr. Case,' 'the truly Noble and Ingenious Jacob, Lord Astley,' this with reference to a gift of thighbones, 'the Reverend and universally learned Dr. Bathurst,' and the Dean of Wells, 'one of the most cordial Encouragers of this *design*,' both of whom lent him stones.

There is one glimpse of the doctor at work. He has defined himself in place and time with an exactitude that allows us to look in through the study window and see him at work, quill in hand. He is writing of the Triumvirates of the Stars, dabbling, I fear, in a little astrology. That his conscience is slightly troubled by this leaning towards the dark arts is clear, for he observes, regarding the Signs of the Times, 'it were easy to adapt a triumvirate to ours: But my Religion, and that God hath exhorted us, *not to be dismayed at the signs of Heaven*, and solemnly profess, that 'tis even He *that frustrates the tokens of the lyars, and makes the Diviners mad,* has taught me to forbear.'

He forbears, but his reluctance is clear. Let us not

chide him. Even in this year of grace and wireless broadcasting a large daily newspaper devotes a column to astrology and advises Harry and Harriette on the propitious moment for purchasing a house or having an operation.

Dr. Plot, despite a devout mind, is intrigued by the state of the stars. Hear him.

And indeed this had been all I thought I should have mentioned concerning the Heavens, but that even now while I am writing this, at *Oxon:* on the 23rd of *November, Anno* 1675, about seven at night, behold the Moon set her Bow in the clouds, of a white colour and well determined, which continued so for about half an hour after I first saw it.

I do not propose to follow Dr. Plot in all his fascinating investigations. They were too many and curious. He was interested in tempests and Visitations, in 'Animals, Plants and the universal furniture of the World,' in 'extravagancies and defects occasioned by the exuberancy of matter, or obstinancy of impediments,' as in *Monsters,* in Echoes and Earths, in the Air, the Waters, in Stones, Plants, Brutes, Men and Women, including the sympathetic birth pangs of husbands, in Giants, Omens of Death, in Arts, including cisterns, closets and glass making, in Agriculture and Antiquities, in short, in everything that came to the notice of the industrious and ingenious doctor.

Dr. Plot settled one troublesome matter for me. Serious differences of opinion had arisen between Louis and myself about mileage. The speedometer of my car seldom agreed with the old milestones on the road, and neither of these agreed with the Official Survey maps. There arose the most heated arguments over the distances between places. We could never agree. That well-known mark out of Henley, called the Fairmile, always seemed to me a most unfair mile on foot. The speedometer and the map were also at variance.

But Dr. Plot settled all that. Let him be a warning to amateur cartographers and hikers. He writes of the map in his book:

As for the scale of miles, there being three sorts in Oxfordshire, the greater, the lesser and middle miles, as almost everywhere else; it is contrived according to the middle sort of them; for these I conceive may be most properly called the true Oxfordshire miles, which upon actual dimensuration at several places, I found to contain for the most part nine furlongs and a quarter, of which about 60 answer a Degree.

When I discovered this paragraph the obstinate Louis was in France, doing his *Service Militaire*. I marked it out and saved it for his return, and on reading it he was dumb—"I think I shall never understand the English. *C'est incroyable!*"

But Dr. Plot is so often *incroyable*. He could not hear any echo without desiring to analyse it. He seems to have gone all over Oxfordshire, shouting in the hope of hearing his voice thrown back at him again. Early in the book he announces his intention. 'It will not be amiss to present the Reader with some of

the sports of Nature, and entertain him a while with
the Nymph *Echo;* a Mistress she is, indeed, that is easily
spoke with, yet known to few.'

After that, Dr. Plot carries on with the Nymph in all
sorts of places. He finds three kinds of echo, the
polysyllabical, tonical and manifold. I do not wonder
the farmers looked askance. Although he does not
tell us, it is highly probable the countryside thought
him a little mad, for he went chasing his nymph,
crying—

> *Quae nec reticere loquenti,*
> *Nec prior ipsa loqui didicit resonabilis Echo.*

She answered him in the day only by the last verse,
'but in the night by about twelve of the clock, I
could almost hear the last word of the former verse—
loquenti.' He found the place of this nocturnal echo,
or the *Centrum phonicum,* as he calls it, below the corner of a wall enclosing some hayricks near Chaucer's
house at Woodstock.

His Echo seems to have been a devout nymph.
Lord Bacon had observed that the Nymph had difficulty with the letter S. Dr. Plot sadly reports the
readiness of his nymph to use the wicked name—
Satan.

Hereupon I tried, as well as his Lordship, with
the word *Satan,* beside many others of the same
initial, but found the Echo here neither so modest or
frighted but that, though the Devil has been busy
enough here about, it would readily make use of his
name.

There was something the doctor recalled to my mind with a shock. A few weeks after I had bought my cottage, Mrs. Meek, referring to some rumour of war in the morning paper, said ominously, "We'll soon know, sir, if that spring runs."

"What spring?" I asked.

"Haven't you heard of the Assenden Spring, sir? Why, it'll come right in here. It floods them down in Henley."

"But what has it to do with a war?" I asked.

"It always begins running just before a war, sir. It's an omen."

I began to learn a little more about the omen. Outside my hedge, by the roadside, I discovered that a deep trench had been cut, and bridged at intervals. This, I learned, was a new device to carry the Assenden Spring when it was in flood. There really was a mysterious spring five miles away up in the Chilterns, and a firm local belief that it runs just before the outbreak of war. Thus the flooding of my garden is bound up with the functioning of the League of Nations, or the pact of Locarno, and I do not feel very safe. But there has been a war since I inhabited the cottage, Japan fought China over Manchuria, and the spring did not run. This may, of course, be due to the spring's concern with the white races only.

Now although every day, when I go out, I walk alongside the dyke cut to take the overflow, I had completely forgotten this mysterious spring. But Dr. Plot knew all about it, and there, on page 30, he reminded me of its existence and capriciousness:

'. . . that of Assenton, near Henly-upon-Thames,

is one of the most eminent that I know of in England;
and no question is the same mentioned by Johannes
Euseb. Nierembergius in his book *The Miracles of
Nature*—In Britanniae territorio Chiltrensi sunt fontes
multi, etc.' I suppose he must mean the Chiltern
country of Oxfordshire. 'There are many Springs,
which in fertile years are always dry; but before any
defect, as the Harbingers of an approaching dearth, the
waters get loose, and, as it were breaking prison, they
quickly unite into a forcible stream. And so they did
lately, in An. 1674 with that violence, that several Mills
might have been driven with the Current; and had not
the town of Henly made some diversion for them, their
Fair Mile must have been drowned for a considerable
time.'

After that I could have no doubt. There was a
spring, and war or no war, it had flowed for certainty
in 1674. I have not yet seen it flow, and if legend be
true, I hope I shall not. For once Dr. Plot does not
favour local gossip. 'But the certain natural principal
of such Springs, altogether depending upon a certain
cause, no heed is to be given to such kind of stories,
they being equally as vain as the persons that broached
them.'

It is impossible for me to go out for a walk in any
direction without being reminded of the learned
Dr. Plot. In passing farmyards and fields I had noticed
how fond the local farmers were of hoisting the stacks
above the ground. In the Midlands they are generally
built straight up from the earth. Here around me I
have noticed the stacks often stand on what might be
termed stone toadstools, on which foundation beams

are laid. This leaves a space between the stack and the ground. I could only surmise that it was for the purpose of keeping the corn or hay from ground damp.

But Dr. Plot was quick to discover a much fuller purpose in these stones. They were to preserve the stacks from rats and mice. He noticed that the toadstools were composed of two stones, 'the standers being four obelisks about two feet high and the caps as many hemispherical stones placed upon them with the flat sides downwards.' It was thus impossible for a rat ascending the upright to surmount the overhanging flat tables.

It was natural that Dr. Plot should be interested in the wells of the district. They are common among these cottages. One of the first thrills of Pilgrim Cottage was its sixty-foot deep well, with a beautiful brick interior. The well head, with bucket and windlass, standing under the apple tree, gave just the right rustic note. When I first inhabited the cottage a party of friends who descended upon me insisted on tasting the sparkling water. Down went the bucket and we all drank, declaring we had never tasted such excellent water. The bucket went down a second time.

"Perhaps it's medicinal," said Bernard.

"We'd live longer if we drank well water," observed Charles.

"And keep our school-girl complexions," cried Vicky.

"Well, my dear, I don't think you need——" I began.

I did not finish the sentence. Frantic signals were coming from the kitchen window. Had Mrs. Meek burnt the joint?

I went to the window, full of apprehension.

"Yes, Mrs. Meek?"

"Oh, sir, excuse me calling you, but I don't think them young ladies and gentlemen ought to drink that well water."

"But it's lovely, Mrs. Meek!"

"Well, sir, perhaps you don't know, sir, but all the kitchen and bathwater's drained into the well. You see, when the water was laid on, sir, and the bath was put in, they thought it a good idea to run the waste into the well, as it wasn't wanted any more. I 'ope you don't mind me telling you, sir? And lunch's ready, sir."

I went back to my friends. Lunch was ready. No, I decided it was better not to spoil lunch with Mrs. Meek's revelation. But I was anxious for a few hours concerning the medicine.

There is a sad story connected with my well. We had been troubled by a rat that was captured at last. We decided the best thing was to drown the rat in the well. So Louis deposited the cage on the lawn while he went to find a rope with which to lower it down the well. Alas, when he returned the cage was empty. It had been put down on a tilt, the trap door had swung back and the rat popped out.

A whole week passed before the rat was again trapped. This time we were not going to be fooled. We attached the rope with the greatest care and marched to the well. But that rat was not destined to die by drowning, for when I raised the lid of the well I was dismayed to find that the whole of the brick lining had collapsed and had filled the well to the level of the water. To rebuild the disused well would have been too expensive. I had to fill it up at a cost of four pounds. But I have retained the well head both for its rustic note and as a memorial to a well that, having lasted some hundreds of years, chose to collapse within a month of my advent.

The countryside is still full of well stories. Within a few hundred yards there are six cottages sharing a well, although not fifty yards distant from them there is a water supply. Yet such are red tape and official preciosity, water cannot be carried those fifty yards across territory beyond the water company's boundary.

Strange things happened in Dr. Plot's day when men went down wells. They sent forth, he tells us, 'such sudden and deadly steams,' and he narrates how two men, digging a well, 'sank down and irrecoverably dyed,' and a miller, being called to assist, he too 'dyed.' But he has a sadder story, dated the 20th August, 1674. A woman who had let fall her bucket called a lusty strong man to go down by a ladder to fetch it up.

He soon granted her unhappy request; for by that time he came half-way down, he fell dead from the ladder into the water; the woman amazed, calls another of her Neighbours, a lusty young man of about eight and twenty, who, hastily descending to give his assistance, much about the same place also fell from the ladder, and dyed, without giving the least sign of his change, so suddenly mortal are the damps of this *earth*.

Sad, indeed, but a doctor of many years' practice in the locality has a story of as strange an happening as anything Dr. Plot had report of. A few miles distant from me there is a large park belonging to an old mansion. The children of the house had a favourite donkey, and when he was not wanted as their companion he was turned loose amid the deer. One day, on being required, the donkey was missing. A long search was unavailing. The lodge-keeper was closely questioned, and was emphatic that no one had taken the donkey out of the park. The game-keepers, the police and the peasantry were warned, a handsome reward was offered, but the pet donkey was never found and his disappearance remained a mystery.

The years passed and the incident was forgotten. Then some thirty years later, repairs being necessary to the large well in the keeper's garden, workmen descended, and the mystery was solved. They found at the bottom the skeleton of a donkey.

"But," I expostulated, when the doctor told me the story, "wasn't the lodge-keeper poisoned?"

"No, not at all, and he brought up a family of five healthy children."

"You're not suggesting the children were healthy because——"

"Oh no," he interrupted, laughing. "You know the old saying—'What the eye never sees'——"

"—The stomach never feels. Yes, but what an un-professional attitude, doctor!"

"Ah, my dear fellow," replied the old doctor, toying with his port glass, "there's a lot of nonsense talked in the name of Hygiene. Now take rheumatism and damp houses. I've lived around here for seventy years. Some of these cottages have never been dry. You can see water trickle down the thick old walls, and you find people living there, seventy and eighty years old, who hardly know what rheumatism is! I'm all for sanitation and dry cottages—but——"

He raised his glass, looked at it and added—

"And yet I know this'll give me awful twinges to-morrow!"

Dr. Plot, pursuing his enquiries on the wonders of wells and water, must have been thrilled by the strange discovery at Watlington Park, 'belonging to the Worshipful Thomas Stonor, Esq.' This gentleman's pond was being cleaned in July 1675. The workmen emptying it came at last to what proved to be the top branches of an oak. This subaqueous wonder was reported to the worthy Mr. Stonor, 'a person not only curious but equally generous,' who thereupon engaged more men and sunk a pit twenty yards wide and sixty deep. They found many whole oaks 'whereof one stood upright perpendicular to the Horizon, the others lay obliquely, only one was inverted, the forked end downwards. All of them dyed through of a black hiew like Ebony.'

We will pass over the doctor's hair-raising investi-gations of ghostly visitations, knockings, the throwing about of furniture, the snatching of bed-clothes off the frighted householders. But an exception must be made concerning the strange happenings at the Manor House, Woodstock, on the night of the 29th October, 1649. The Commissioners of Survey were lodging in the house. They were probably unpopular, but even so they scarcely justified the terrors rained upon them so copiously that, after five nights, they fled to Ewelme.

I should find myself a little incredulous of Dr. Plot had he not been at the greatest pains to find and examine reputable eye-witnesses. He confesses for himself that he 'has no esteem for such stories' and yet——

We will read of the night of the 29th October. Records the Doctor:

Something walked in the withdrawing-room about an hour, and going to the window, opened and shut it, then going to the bedchamber, it threw great stones for about half an hour's time, somewhereof lighted on the high-bed, and others on the truckle-bed, to the number in all of about four-score. This night there was also a very great noise, as though forty pieces of Ordnance had been shot off together . . . both Commissioners and servants were struck with so great horror that they cryed out to one another for help, whereof one of them recovering himself out of a strange agony he had been in, snatched up a sword and had liked to have killed one of his Brethren coming out of his bed in his shirt, whom he took for the Spirit that did the mischief. However,

at length they all got together, yet the noise continued so great and terrible, and they shook the walls
so much, that they thought the whole manor would
have fell on their heads.   At its departure it took all
the glass away with it.

Immediately after the *Visitations* Dr. Plot turns to
unusual diseases, and records 'A Ranula under the
tongue, wherein there bred a stone' in the mouth of
Mr. Evans, the Rector of Heath; a stone out of the
bladder of Mr. Skringley 'weighing about a pound,
and being ten inches round one way, and full eleven
the other'; a corn that grew on the toe of one Sarney,
a wheelwright, in the city of Oxford, Anno 1655,
'two inches long which, for the unusual figure and
bigness of it, I have caused to be ingraven of its just
magnitude.'

Only once does the amazing doctor appear to be
'flummoxed.'   In the birth of man, he observes, it is
equally strange 'that the pangs of the woman in the
exclusion of the child have sometimes affected the Ab-
domen of the husband, which yet to such as have experimented the secrecy of sympathies, and understand
the subtilty and power of effluviums, perhaps may not
seem difficult.'

But the fact that these birth pangs were felt by husbands in Oxfordshire mystifies Dr. Plot.

That the man should sometimes suffer such pains,
whilst the woman is well, is a problem, I fear,
beyond all hopes of solution.   And yet this has
happened to some persons in Oxfordshire is very

certain, and that to knowing ones too, very likely to be undeceived.

The learned doctor examined a number of victims, and

> One of them told me that they came upon him when he little thought of his wife, and that the pangs were very odd ones, such as he never felt in his life; not like any *griping* in the *guts,* but lying in the muscles of the Abdomen, which yet he should never have thought to have had relation to his wife had they not suddenly ceased as soon as his wife began to be in *labor.*

But let us turn, with Dr. Plot, from gynæcology to glass.

He had yet another revelation which made clear a problem in my mind. My dining-room window is divided into small panes. I noticed that one of the lower panes was faulty and distorted everything seen through it. I thought of having some new glass put in, when I happened to point out the old pane to my ancient gardener.

"Ay—it's fair crizelled, it is! There's a lot o' that about here—it's home-made."

"Crizelled?" I repeated.

"Yes—all wobbly-like, sir."

I retreated indoors and searched the dictionaries. Crizelled was evidently a local word, it could not be found in my books. And 'home-made'—did he really mean the glass was made at home? Further enquiries elicited the information that Henley had once had a glass industry, but no one seemed to know why the glass was crizelled.

There the matter would have ended, but Dr. Plot again revealed his omniscience. He knew all about it and turned from Spirits to Glass with equal readiness of information. What was there he did not know?

There was, he says, 'the invention of making Glasses of stones and some other materials, at Henly on Thames, lately brought into England by Seignior de Costa a Montferratees.'

The materials used were the local black flints that one finds used in the walls of the houses in the Chiltern district. These were calcined, and mixed with white sand. The ingenious Dr. Ludwell, Fellow of Wadham College, found a solution by adding two ounces of nitre, tartar and borax.

But the Glasses made of these being subject to that unpardonable fault called Crizelling, caused by the two great quantities of Salt in the mixture . . . and thereby endure a Scabrities or dull roughness, irrecoverably clouding the transparency of the glass.

The memory of the octogenarian once more had proved a reliable transmitter of local tradition. I knew now why the old gardener said my window was "fair crizelled." It was the old Henley glass, from the process of Seignior de Costa a Montferratees. Dr. Plot, of course, was not content with this bare statement. He wanted to know all about the local glass industry. Since it is now extinct, his enquiries are interesting. He continues:

They have chosen rather since to make their glasses of a great sort of white pebbles, which, as I am informed, they have from the River Po in Italy. . . . They now make a sort of Pebbleglass, which are hard, durable, and whiter than any from Venice, and will not Crizel, but endure the severest trials whatever, to be known from the former by a Seal set purposely on them.

Never again do I complain when the view is obscured by my crizelled glass. I feel grateful for the industry founded by Seignior de Costa a Montferratees. I have looked in vain, however, for a piece of that later glass with a seal on it which, in the good doctor's eyes, seemed an improvement on any from Venice. But I fear local patriotism led him astray in this matter. They still make Venetian glass at Murano, but the glass-making industry has long been dead at Henley.

In the chapter of Dr. Plot's investigations among 'Arts that concern formation of Earths,' he alludes to the making of 'Tobacco-pipes of the White-earth of Shot-over,' our old friends the churchwardens, doubtless. He notes that 'the ingenious John Dwight, M.A., hath discovered the *mystery* of the stone or Cologne Wares, such as D'Alva Bottles, Jugs, Noggins,' and following his dissertation on crizel glass, proceeds 'to the *Arts* relating to *Plants*.'

It is to the glory of the ingenious Dr. Plot that he always lives up to his name. In everything he narrates there is an astonishing surprise. He could never have foreseen, for instance, that I, a reader of his book, two hundred and fifty years after his death, should have a strange weakness for the toucan. Ever since I first saw that gorgeous bird, with its preposterous crimson beak, I have hankered after one. There is something as absurd in the name as in the bird, which so out-parrots the parrot. I never for a moment expected that Dr. Plot had heard of this tropical bird so dear to my heart. But bless him, he had. He had not only heard of it, he knew all about it, and had seen one in Oxfordshire!

But what is somewhat stranger, in the year 1644, the *Pica Brasiliensis,* or Toucan, whose beak is near as big as its whole body, was found within two miles of Oxford, and given to the Repository in the Medecine-School, where it is still to be seen; which argues it a Bird of a very *rank* wing, there being a necessity of its flying from America hither, except that we shall rather say it might be brought into England by Ship, and afterwards getting away might fly hither.

If anything more had been required to endear me to Dr. Plot that paragraph would have sufficed.

That he would tell me something I did not know when he turned 'to the Arts relating to Plants,' I had no doubt. I was not disappointed. Although, unlike his friend, the learned and accurate Dr. Grew, he was not 'now reading, writing and practising the Anatomy of Vegetables,' there was little in field or garden that escaped his inquisitive mind.

Dr. Plot thought it not unreasonable that some plants

produced different colours from the rest of their spe-
cies.   He observed that they were as strong and flourished as well as any others.   'Why then,' he asks indignantly, 'should they be numbered among diseased
plants, any more than a red-haired man should be
accounted so in England, or a black-hair'd one in Den-
mark, where I am informed there are so few that they
commonly paint Judas with black hair as we do
with red.'

But the learned doctor did startle me with his information upon perspiring plants.   He tells us of an
experiment made in June, 1669, by a worthy friend in
order to find in what measure plants might perspire.
This gentleman took two narrow glasses and filled each
with one pound, eight ounces, two drachms of water.
In one of these filled glasses he put a sprig of mint
weighing one ounce.   He exposed both glasses in a
window to the sun.   After ten days he found in the
glass holding the mint only five ounces and four
drachms of water, so that one pound two ounces and
six drachms had disappeared.   The mint, be it noted,
weighed less than two drachms more than at first.

From the other glass, without mint, one ounce of
water had evaporated.   It was assumed that a similar
quantity had been evaporated in each by the sun, and
that therefore the mint had absorbed in ten days one
pound, one ounce, six drachms of water.   Since it had
only increased in weight two drachms it was clear that
the mint

had purely expired in those ten days, one pound,
one ounce and four drachms; that is, each day about

an ounce and a half, which is more than the weight of the whole mint. Whence he concluded that what Malpighius so wonders at in his book *De Bombyce*, viz. that those Animals will sometimes eat in one day more than the weight of their bodies, is outdone by every sprig of mint.

Now, notwithstanding Malpighius, whoever he might be, I refused to believe that a sprig of mint weighing one ounce could in ten days imbibe and cast off one pound, one ounce and four drachms, that is, seventeen times its own weight! There is no drunkard in history who could equal that record no matter how he perspired. I was sadly compelled to think that Dr. Plot had had his leg pulled by a too ingenious friend. In all the astonishing facts he had brought to light, so far as they could be checked, by observation or tradition, the doctor was strictly truthful and painstakingly cautious. Could he be right about the mint? I decided to test the matter for myself. I procured two glasses such as are used for bulb culture. I filled each with one pound eight ounces of water. I then selected a sprig of mint weighing one ounce and put it in one of the glasses, placing both in a sunny window. After ten days, I measured in the mint glass five ounces and a drachm of water, so that one pound, two ounces, seven drachms of water had disappeared. The mint had not appreciably changed in weight. The water in the other glass had evaporated one ounce four drachms, therefore the mint had absorbed in ten days one pound, one ounce and three drachms, or one ounce and three-quarters per day!

I wore the sprig in my lapel all that day in honour of Dr. Plot.

And now we must leave Dr. Plot, to go into the garden, where a Hunt puppy from across the way has just been caught digging up a bed of grape hyacinths. I have placed the learned doctor's volume on the book-shelf by the fireplace. It looks handsome there, and will be an honoured guest in the cottage library. I shall return again and again to Dr. Plot, for the erudi-tion he displays, for his quaint and courtly style, for the pleasure of turning the large yellowed pages of handset type. He has left a clear picture of himself, seated at his desk, in Oxford, when the Moon set her Bow in the clouds. He bids us farewell with character-istic modesty and dignity:

And thus with no small toil and charge, yet not without the assistance of many Honorable Persons, whose names in due time shall be all gratefully men-tioned, I have made shift to finish this specimen of Oxfordshire: which I am far from taking for a perfect History, that I doubt not that time and severe observation may produce an Appendix as large as this book.

Alas! The book passed into a second edition, but before that happy endorsement of his labours, the learned doctor had himself passed into another world, where doubtless his curiosity is endlessly exercised, and much that puzzled him is revealed.

GHOSTLY NOISES

Strange sounds are heard about the house at midnight,
   In the hall and on the stair,
They are so furtive and so apprehensive,
   And they come upon you unaware,
That you wonder whether they were inmates
   Long ago, or from ghostly tread
Of the great-grandfather on the wall there
   When he took a tallow candle and went creeping up
    to bed.

CHAPTER XIV

OCTOGENARIA

I

I HAD not dwelt long in the country before I found myself becoming a collector of octogenarians. Old houses, old furniture, old trees and old people are the true representatives of country life, I discovered. Within a two-mile radius of my cottage I had come to know and pass pleasant hours with no less than eleven old folk, all ranging in age from eighty to ninety-five. They all had prodigious memories, and were full of content. That they thought the world had gone mad I did not doubt, but it was a lunacy that filled their days with speculation. Sometimes the rush of the age carried them off their feet. There was old Mr. Bowler, aged eighty-four, whom I first discovered drinking his seventh pint in the parlour of *The Rainbow*, an inn that surpasses my own *Golden Ball* for rustic charm. I sometimes call there at the end of a long walk on the hills. It sits in the valley on my homeward road, smiling across a pleasant garden, with triple dormer windows and red tiles, as on my own dwelling.

Mr. Bowler, I discovered, was a local character. He still worked as a labourer in the fields, and, like old Charlie the bell-ringer, he could remember earning two shillings a day, with a shilling on Sunday as a birdscarer. It took me some time to understand his speech

owing to his toothless condition, and an Oxfordshire
accent in all its richness, but when at last I mastered
it and overcame his suspicion, I found him a mine of
information, with astonishing shrewdness and plain
sense.   His father had lived to ninety-four and had seen
three of his fellow farm-labourers hanged at Abingdon
for taking part in the riots and rick burnings that pre-
ceded the Reform Bill.   Thus Mr. Bowler's father had
narrowly escaped being deported along with thirty labourers sentenced to transportation for life.   "An' I
might 'eve been born an Australian, I might!" said
Mr. Bowler, with a chuckle.

He would not have it that there had been any good
old days.   "But ye wasn't un'appy, let me say.   They
didn't give ye time to think about it."   Mr. Bowler
lived in the cottage where he was born.   The rent was
two shillings.   It was kept by a widowed daughter
with a son.   The doings of Mr. Bowler's grandson were
epical.   The youth had made a wireless set and he
owned a motor-cycle.   He worked at a local wood-
yard.   Once a week he took his grandad on the back
of his cycle to the cinema in Henley.   The old man
loved the ride and 'the pictures,' and no fear of his
daughter could stop him sitting astride the carrier and
going off, swaying behind the back of the youth at forty
miles an hour.

The wireless also raised alarm.   For years Mr. Bowler
had gone to bed at nine.   Now he insisted on sitting up
after ten, because he could hear dance music relayed
from London.   He did not dance, but he liked jazz—
"It's got summat in it," he explained to me.

One mellow October afternoon when I was up a ladder picking apples, I heard a woman's voice in the road say, "I'm taking it to my mother—it's her birthday to-morrow." I could not see what 'it' was, but I recognised the voice as belonging to a middle-aged woman who often passed my gate.

"How old is she?" I called out to the woman hidden by the hedge.

There was a silence following the surprise at this voice coming from the upper air, then she answered:

"Ninety-two, sir!"

"Can she go out?"

"Just a little."

"Then if it's a nice day to-morrow, tell her I'll come and take her out in the car."

Thus I added a nonagenarian to the octogenarians.

I thought at first she might prove to be the old lady who took a morning walk past my door, but she was not. Every morning when I lay reading or writing on the sun platform I would hear slow steps coming along 'the Roman road.' I got into the habit of looking over and greeting the old lady, wrapped in a shawl, who walked so slowly down my lane. Occasionally she was accompanied by a young woman, more often she was alone. Then for a few days I missed her.

Making enquiries at an adjacent cottage, I learned that she had lost her husband, a man of eighty-six, after sixty-four years of married life. I had occasionally greeted him sitting at a door gay with the blossom of japonica. The village cemetery is just visible from my platform, and I can hear the interment bell toll. I was leaving for London one afternoon when I heard the bell. In the country this solemn note breaks in upon one's preoccupation with life. In the city Birth and Death lose their significance amid the unheeding rush. They come to the house next door or the flat above with about as much inconsequence to the neighbours as the laundry delivery van.

For a moment I paused at the wheel of my car, giving ear to the solemn bell tolling for the funeral of the old man who had so often wished me 'Good day' at his cottage door. Then I departed for London, pressed for time. I returned six days later, and as I was about to turn my car into the lane I was aware of a small gathering of solemn folk at the cottage opposite. In a moment I knew what had happened in Nature's kindly dispensation. They were carrying the old lady across the road into the quiet field where her partner of sixty-four years had waited so short a time.

> *They were lovely and pleasant in their lives*
> *And in death they were not divided.*

It is a lovely epitaph with which to close a long pilgrimage.

II

My old friend Mrs. Harman, the blacksmith's wife, had heard I was writing a book about the country. There was scarcely a phase of my activities in the literary world of which she was not aware. Exiled in a village of the Chilterns, with neither train nor omnibus service, she always knew, nevertheless, about my latest book or public appearance. I once slyly wrote an article all about her and the blacksmith. It was published in an American paper. I said nothing about it, not wishing to embarrass them by the complimentary terms in which I had written of them, though disguised in name and place. One day when I called, the door was opened and a face wreathed in smiles greeted me.

"Oh, sir, we're so glad you've come. We've read your article, and we feel so flattered! Just fancy being in print!" exclaimed the old lady.

I affected surprise, but it was useless. My article confronted me on the cottage table. A married niece in Philadelphia had recognised the originals and sent it to them. Reviews of my books seemed to come into Mrs. Harman's hands, no matter where they appeared. Her interest did not end there. I have taken a long list of distinguished friends there, to enjoy the lively intelligence of the blacksmith and his wife, to view the old smithy, the large cat, and the panorama of woods and valleys from the window. Whatever they wrote or did was thereafter noted by Mrs. Harman. Our conversation invariably opened with a discussion of some book they had just written and she had read. Town people may find the country 'dead,' but anyone with knowledge of the country knows how many and lively are the unseen lines of communication with the outer world, where noise and alertness are mistaken for intelligence.

Mrs. Harman, with an idea of providing material for my country chronicle, said, "You must visit old Charlie, sir—and also Mr. Rixon, the last of the chairmakers."

"The last of the chair-makers?" I repeated in surprise.

Not many miles distant, in High Wycombe, there were factories devoted to the business of chair-making. The great beechwoods of the Chilterns were being devastated by this growing industry. Happily they had not been able to encroach upon the large estate in my own district, where miles of noble woods had been spared the axe.

I was taken to call at a thatched cottage beyond the village green, and received a warm welcome from the chair-maker and his wife. He was a little old man of eighty-one with a bright eye and an impish face. I thought of the bored young men one encounters around club bars, who wonder at thirty how they will continue to get through the next twelve months. The old man was so alert, and had so many facts of interest to impart, that I had to pin him down question by question.

He shocked me a little by the delight with which he produced a newly turned leg of a chair. His grandson had taken him to a furniture factory in High Wycombe, and had shown him a German lathe. Would I believe it, asked the old man excitedly, fifty chair-legs had been turned out in one minute, and they had lathes to make a thousand an hour! He pointed out, with a pride that sprang from his own craftsmanship, that the lathe making such a leg must have had at least seven chisels. "Why, it would 'ave tekken me half an' hour to do it. That machine's better than thirty of us!"

Now you would have expected, in the face of this

evidence of machine versus man, the old chair-maker would have been indignant or sad at this abolition of ancient craftsmanship. I tried to suggest that a hand-turned leg must be better than one machined, but he would not agree. That machine was wonderful. The eagerness in the old fellow's face told me he envied his grandson working in such a factory of wonders.

His wife had now produced half a dozen old chairs. Some were made of cherry wood, some of beech. They were all polished by long use, and beautiful in their curves, proclaiming craftsmanship of the highest order. The old chair-maker explained how they had been made, and took me out to a shed at the bottom of his orchard to show me the lathe on which the work had been done.

I had to repress my laughter on seeing the crazy old apparatus he called a lathe. It was entirely home-made. The bench was some boards knocked together. The two poppet-heads for holding the turning were fastened by hammering wedges into a groove, and each poppet had an iron pin that was jammed into the piece of wood for turning. This part of the lathe was primitive enough, but the power for driving it was even more primitive. A sapling growing in the garden was bent down, and a cord from this passed around the future chair-leg and was connected to a strip of wood that acted as a treadle. On pressing the treadle down the springy sapling made the cord taut and revolved the chair-leg. The turning was done on the down stroke, which revolved the leg towards the worker. Despite the jim-crack nature of these pole-lathes, as they were called, a skilled worker could turn out four dozen legs an hour.

There was one feature in which this kind of turning was better than machine turning. To-day, the wood must go to the factory; before, the lathe went to the wood. It was the habit of the chair-maker to buy a 'fall' of beech, and set up his lathe at the side of the trunk, sawing off and splitting piece by piece as he needed it. The old chair-maker showed me a photograph of half a dozen turners sitting by their machines in the heart of the wood.

I asked him if there were any chair-makers working the pole-lathe now.

"Only a few. Them machines in Wycombe's killed 'em all. They won't know what a pole-lathe is in ten years. I reckon that lathe o' mine ought to go in a museum an' me with it!"

He gave a chuckle at this. His grandson, smartly dressed for the town, wheeled a motor-cycle out of the yard and started it up with a roar.

"That's what everybody wants nowadays—they won't want chairs at all soon, they'll have forgotten how to sit!"

I left him in front of the fire, his wife dressing the clothes-horse. The firelight fell on their cheerful old faces, and on the chairs shining with fifty years of use. In one corner a tall narrow baby chair with guard rail and step had long been deserted. The cat now slept in it.

Old Charlie was next visited, he who had rung the church bells for fifty years alongside Mark Harman. He had a face like a wrinkled walnut set in a fringe of

white whiskers. If the chair-maker was an imp, the
old bell-ringer was a gnome.   He rose from his presentation chair to greet me in a cottage set in an orchard, with a grand view of the Berkshire hills.   The
view had not changed since the day he had been born
in this cottage, eighty-six years ago.   At the end of
the garden there were some tall walnut trees he had
planted when a boy.

The moment I entered I was conscious of an air of
excitement.   Tea was laid on the cottage table, and the
niece of the grand old bachelor bustled to get me a
chair.   Then a visiting nephew appeared and the excitement was explained.   He had bought his uncle a
wireless cabinet.   The old man, who could remember
rushlights, and his grandmother, at eighty, going with
yoke and pails to fetch water from a spring a mile and
a half away, had just been listening to a concert in
Paris.   But when Big Ben chimed the hour, he glanced
at the clock on the mantelpiece and said, severely, "That
ain't right!"

He was a grand declaimer.   Worked up by dramatic
emotion when telling a story, he often rose to his feet
and made the rafters ring.   He was still full of enthusiasm for life and climbed his trees to gather apples.
As with so many of these old people, life was sustained
by the old-age pension, contributions from relations, and
a negligible rent to the squire.

During one of the conversations upon old times I
discovered the reason of a local enthusiasm for tiles
and a disparagement of thatch, so beloved by the city
man.   Those who lived under tiles collected the rain-
water in tanks.   The rain on thatch could not be col-

lected. It had to be transported from the pond by the church. In deep winter, of course, one just stepped out and collected a canful of snow! No wonder I found no enthusiasm among the octogenarians for the good old days!

The beauty of the countryside is rapidly disappearing under the anarchy of the speculative builder. The farms of England, once a source of her strength and prosperity, are falling into ruin, while queues of dejected men wait at Labour Exchanges. But there is no lament among the greybeards for the good old days! They prefer the conveniences that have come in with economic instability, and the entertainment that surrounds them at the price of noise. Mrs. Harman remembers journeying between squire, vicar and schoolmaster, with the one newspaper they shared. To-day all read and enjoy the paper, even while they believe it is mostly lies.

But the greybeards have one lament: they regret the disappearance of the squire, who was not the ogre of the indignant Radical, but almost always the father of his people.

THE SQUIRE

If Squire lived well, dressed well, travelled,
    Can it be denied
Among all breeds of Englishmen
    He was England's pride?

If he ruled hard, rough in justice,
    Was it ever said
He took a proffered bribe,
    His honour dead?

If he lived in comfort, slept well,
    He bred brave sons,
Who faced with dauntless courage
    The deadly guns.

If the Hall was his, the Living,
    The whole estate,
He knew the name of each **man**
    About his gate.

But these new lords who traffic
    In Stock and Share,
Whom else do they profit
    Playing 'bull' or 'bear'?

Ten thousand soaring shares sold
    On a rise of 'twenty,'
To how many cottages bring they
    Food in plenty?

If Squire rode hard, swore hard, drank hard,
    Let the truth be said,
He farmed five thousand **acres**,
    He gave England bread.

CHAPTER XV

COTTAGE SECRETS

I

I was busy trimming the privet hedge that hides my cottage from the lane when a small boy of six dismounted a toy cycle and watched me with interest. I decided to wait for him to open the conversation. I had not to wait long, but I was startled by his opening question.

"Are you the author?" he asked with complete candour.

I turned and looked at the small boy in a lilac blouse and corduroy shorts.

"Yes—I suppose I am," I confessed.

He looked at me more critically, and I had a feeling that I did not satisfy his expectations.

"I suppose you are very rich—you make a lot of money writing books?" he asked gravely.

This startling aspect of the literary life, and of myself as a man of wealth, left me without an answer for a space. So I took the defensive and asked questions. He was visiting the doctor's son across the way, and was a doctor's son himself. Was his question, with its suggestion of easy wealth, an echo from my neighbour's conversation in front of this small boy?

It is flattering to learn, even from a child's mind, that one is regarded as a rich man. I stopped clipping and began to wonder at what point of painful accumulation

an author can consider himself rich.   I had spent the
previous week-end at a house that had terraces a quarter
of a mile long, an Italian cypress grove, a covered riding
school and a large lake.   These were oddments among
assets of perfect hospitality.   Yet I am sure my host
would have been alarmed if someone had informed him
that he was a rich man, despite the additional possession
of a yacht and a mansion in town.   It is rarely one meets
a man who will admit he is rich.   Once, for a few heady
weeks, I moved in an atmosphere of American million-
aires.   They were all obsessed with the elusiveness of
money.

My young visitor next expressed a wish to see my
house.

"I hear it's funny," he said, with his disarming candour.

As I took him over it, he expressed so much approval
that I began to feel he might take it at eight guineas a
week.   He asked to go upstairs.   In the large bedroom
with its twin beds, Aged Six asked me if I was married.
When I said "No," he asked, "Then who sleeps in the
other bed?"

I hustled the young man downstairs.   And yet that
question shows the very direct working of a child's mind.
Doubtless at home his parents occupied twin beds.   It
was a logical question for Aged Six.   Fifteen years
hence, when preparatory school, public school and Var-
sity have worked their will on his receptive mind, how
much of that inquisition to which I was subjected will
be remembered by him?   Will the 'funny' house have
grown funnier, its owner richer, or will they diminish
in the perspective of Time?

When my young visitor had gone I resumed the clipping of the hedge. But this was to be a morning of interruptions. I was wanted on the telephone. Laying aside the shears I went into the house. It was a pushful young man in a Henley auctioneer and estate agent's firm. Could I see him for a few minutes on urgent business? What business? I asked. Business that was certain to interest me greatly, he replied.

I could not think of any business emerging from an estate agent's that would interest me greatly. I told him so.

"It may affect your property," he said.

Now that is an answer certain to break down any property-owner's resistance. It has the nature of a blow below the belt. The owner of property, however small, is always afraid that something may affect the value or the amenity of his place. This artful young man knew this. Immediately, I had horrid visions of a gasworks in the empty field opposite me, of a sawmill droning at the end of the lane, of a private lunatic asylum established in the very large house they could not sell across the way.

This empty house had a groom's cottage which had been let separately to a man with children who played, in both senses of the word, on a reverberant piano. In summer, with the door open, the sound of *The Maiden's Prayer* invoked a bachelor's curse. Then a kind Fate removed this discord from my ears, and all was peace again. But a menace of this kind had made me apprehensive. 'It may affect your property.' That ominous sentence made me jump. I told the young man I would see him.

I went back to my clipping, but my heart was not in my work, and I almost welcomed his arrival. He produced a great sheaf of papers and some rolled-up plans. His revelation was startling enough, but I felt relieved of personal anxiety. The whole estate that surrounded me, the woods, farms and cottages, were to be sold by auction.

This was lamentable news. For several generations one family had kept intact, and in excellent order, a large estate. They had been proud of their beautiful property, with its magnificent beechwoods clothing the steep hillsides, its plantations of larch and fir, its partridge coverts, its cottages, small-holdings and farms. Now it was all to be thrown into the market, and the despoiling hand of the speculative builder would mar the rustic scene.

The manner of this spoliation was worse than I had feared on first hearing the news. The Squire, oppressed with rising taxation and falling income, had sold his estate outright to a speculator, who would divide it into lots. Already great belts of the beechwoods had been sold for cutting down. In the weeks that followed, as I took my walks in woods that were among the loveliest England could show, ominous rings appeared on trees doomed to fall. But as yet I had no idea of the extent of this callous devastation. Later, the park wall was to be broken down and the dignity of the noble Fairmile, skirting the deer park, was to be shattered by a sporadic growth of villas.

In regard to my own situation the young man was an alarmist, and I firmly declined to have 'the first pick' of bargains in cottages, farms, fields or woods. But it was clear others would have to buy to preserve their amenities.

Dismay spread over the countryside. There was sorrow for the necessity that had compelled a popular family to sell the greater part of a fine estate. There was an outcry against the vandalism of cutting down stretches of glorious woods. Near me were two industrious sisters who rented a small dairy farm. They lived in an old farmhouse fronted by fantastically clipped yews. They grazed some of their cows on the open road, and were familiar figures bringing their cattle home at even. Now, after twenty years, they were at the mercy of the purchaser of their farm. Their livelihood might be wholly threatened.

Up a narrow lane leading to the deer park there was a gamekeeper's lodge. The gamekeeper was discharged, his lodge for sale. I knew and respected the old man. Everyone on the estate was suddenly faced with unemployment, and it was beyond the means of the Squire to provide for all. In the cases of very old tenants he had been able to stipulate that they should enjoy life tenancy at the old rent.

For years I had read of the break up of England's large estates, but never until now had I realised what this entailed in the lives of those who lived on the soil, who were wholly dependent on their small-holdings. I was suddenly made aware of the debt we owe to these disappearing landlords who had preserved intact the great beauty of the landscape, who trimmed hedges, repaired fences and gates, and kept guard over magnificent woodlands.

I was able to allay the fears of the old gamekeeper by

buying his lodge and allowing him to continue his
tenancy.   I immediately had other appeals for help that
unhappily I could not meet.   We all awaited the day
of the public auction in the deepest gloom.   I gave up
some of my walks since I could not endure looking on
so many noble trees marked for execution.

In the first shock of the news I had forgotten my old
friends at the smithy.   Happily they were among those
for whom the Squire had stipulated a life tenancy at
the old rent.   But they were distressed, nevertheless.
They saw the hand of Change grasping all that had
been familiar and dear to them.   They had felt themselves members of a large family, and now they were
only a plot on a plan, offered up in public auction.
Despite their guarantee of tenancy, I saw they were
worried by the prospect of an unknown landlord.   After fifty years of rent paying to the Squire they were
unsettled by the thought of cold eyes examining their
home, and regarding them as obtruders removable only
by death.

I had not intended going to the sale.   The whole
thing was distasteful to me, but curiosity overcame me.
I found nearly a hundred people in the hall.   The
atmosphere was that of an inquest.   There was a good
number of tenants, curious to see to whom they were
to be sold; others, after desperate manœuvres to raise
money, came to attempt a purchase.   There were some
speculative builders, tight-mouthed and suspicious of
each other.   The rest comprised the leisured and the
curious like myself.

A few minutes before the sale began the high table
was filled with important-looking gentlemen rustling

plans and scribbling in catalogues. There was much whispering and paper shuffling. They created an impression of a shady conspiracy, though they were auctioneers, agents and solicitors long renowned in the disposal of noble and noblemen's properties.

I turned to look at the quiet rows behind me, and what I saw there smote my heart. In one of the rows sat the blacksmith and his wife. Dignified as a churchwarden, in his neat black suit, the old man's face had a wistful solemnity. His blue-eyed rosy-cheeked wife, also in her best black, watched the scene with serious face.

It was a minute to three, the hour for the auction. The energetic young fellow who had visited me one day with the news affecting my property caught my eye. His quick intelligence must have seen something there, for he left the high table and came down to me.

"Now can't I persuade you? There's Lot 27—it's a snip, they'll sell for six hundred and fifty. If it goes up for auction it'll fetch eight hundred," he said. "What about it?"

"Then it's your duty to let it go up for auction," I retorted.

He laughed, and bent lower.

"I wanted to do you a good turn. Besides, you're a shrewd man, Mr. Roberts. Look at your cottage, you don't regret that?"

I smiled at his tactics. His future seemed assured. He had a most persuasive manner.

"No," I said firmly. "I've not come to buy."

"They're going like hot cakes—you'll see!"

"I don't see any signs of enthusiasm," I retorted. "You're more likely to be mobbed."

"Well, if you won't, you won't," he sighed.

The auctioneer stood up. The sale would begin soon.

"What do you want for Lot 79," I asked, casually. He named a figure. I offered fifty pounds less.

"I don't think they'll take it, but I'll see."

He hurried off, there was a whispered consultation with the auctioneer and a solicitor. He came back.

"That's all right," he said. "Will you write a cheque for ten per cent.? I can give you a blank cheque——"

"I've got my cheque-book," I answered, pulling it out. "To whom shall I make it?"

"Why," he exclaimed, looking at my cheque-book, "you intended buying all along!"

"Not at all," I answered. "I'm on my way to pay the rates."

He took the cheque and came back with the receipt.

The auctioneer began to read out the conditions of the sale.

Slipping out of my seat, I quietly moved towards the blacksmith and his wife. They leaned forward when they saw I wanted to speak to them.

"I've just bought your cottage. I'm your landlord," I whispered to them.

Never shall I forget the radiant smile that sprang to their grave faces, the warmth with which they grasped the hand of their new landlord. Had I paid twice the price I should have felt justified by the glow of happiness suffusing their fine old faces.

And on cool reflection I found I had obtained a good bargain also.

The sale did not proceed with anything like the gusto prophesied by the young agent. There was a sullen air over the proceedings. A few cottage tenants made an effort to purchase their houses. Some succeeded, others were defeated by the speculator. Many of the lots failed to draw bids, or after a desperate beating up in price were withdrawn. The irony of it all was revealed some months later, when the timber wagons were churning up the lanes, and ugly gaps in the beech-woods marked the ruinous trail of the axe-men. The speculator who had bought the estate and thrown it on the market, unsettling the whole countryside, him-self failed. Some of the estate reverted to the Squire. But a sense of unity and security is for ever gone. The stumps of mutilated giants bear witness in the wood-lands to the passage of the wrecker. There has been a terrible and heartless devastation, and slopes once glori-ous with ash and beech stand riven and naked to the sky.

II

Now that I am the owner of the smithy in which the blacksmith has passed his life, I sometimes stand in it and look at its cobwebbed windows, worn floor and iron-littered bench. The anvil, the bellows and furnace are still there. Hammers, nails and horse-shoes are all around. Occasionally the smithy rings as of old with the wheeze of the bellows, the tapping of iron and a 'whoa!' from a human throat. For a visiting blacksmith comes at intervals to shoe the few remaining horses on the farms. He is watched wistfully by the old man, who remembers rising at dawn and working till sunset to shoe the Squire's horses.

One of his last tasks was his saddest. On the cottage dresser stands the photograph of his only son, the last of the line after more than three hundred years in this small village. The initials of the fallen soldier and of his regiment have been cunningly worked in an iron photograph frame. Elsewhere, on the gates of a large house, and in many a cottage, there are other examples of his ancient craft, for the village blacksmith did much more than shoe horses. His work became part of the daily life of the people, and he supplied many utensils of domestic use.

When you first go to live in an old house you embark on a voyage of discovery. The knocker on the door, its hinges, its latches are all products of the blacksmith's shop. But it is around the fireplace that his craft is visible at its best.

Pilgrim Cottage has yielded up secret after secret. It reserves some mysteries for me still. On the left-hand side of the drawing-room fireplace, about a foot from the ground, there is a cavity some four inches deep with a curved face. The round brick has been cut away or worn away for a purpose we have failed to determine. When I was building the fireplace in the old open grate I discovered up the chimney, some five feet high, a deep pocket in the right-hand wall. What was this for? It could not be seen, it could not be reached without standing up inside the chimney, and getting well sooted. It has been suggested to me, with some reason, that it was a hiding hole for money. Nothing could be more secretive.

Up the chimney I also discovered an iron cross-bar with a chain. This piece of the blacksmith's work was for hanging the pot over the fire. Many of these old chimneys had cranes, bracketed on the side wall. These could be swung out over the fire, and had an ingenious ratchet attachment for lengthening the arm, or heightening and lowering the suspended pot.

The smith made all the utensils for the kitchen. The tongs and fire-shovels of his day have a beauty absent from the modern articles, turned out by the thousand. Nothing could be more delicate and beautiful in its curves than the old hand-tongs used for picking up a brand and blowing it into a flame for lighting a rush or a pipe. I have a pair of old tongs still in use. For a long time I was puzzled by a projecting stud on the shoulder hinging each tongue. Then one day an old blacksmith told me. It was used for stopping tobacco in the churchwarden clay pipes.

In a cupboard at the side of the fireplace, long regarded as a powder cupboard, I found a curious iron article, rather like a pair of nail pliers, but with sharp edges to the nose. Again I was puzzled by this singular but perfect bit of ironwork. Finally I discovered an antiquarian who told me they were sugar nippers. We have all heard of sugar-loaves, but few of us have seen one. In the old days sugar was frequently sold in a large conical lump known as a loaf. Small lumps were nipped off the loaf by these nippers.

There was one discovery above all others that filled my day with excitement. The great fireplace in the

dining-room, once the kitchen, had features that puzzled me greatly.   Over the mantelpiece, about three feet
apart, there were two slotted oak uprights.   At first I
had believed this was a gun-rack.   My supposition was
encouraged by the fact that at the side of the fireplace
there was a little cupboard, with two beautiful old
hinges and scutcheon.   This, I told myself, must be the
powder cupboard for the guns.

The gun-rack theory had one serious drawback.   No
kind of gun I could find would fit the rack, for the butt
was always too large.   Someone suggested it was a whip-
rack to carry a wagoner's whips.   I accepted this theory,
but was not wholly convinced.

Two other details of the fireplace baffled me.   In the
mantelshelf, about six inches from the right end, there
was a slot some two inches long and half an inch wide.
What had this been for?   No one could make a guess.
The nearest explanation I could make was that it had
been cut to hold some kind of ornament.   Then, in
the fireplace itself, there were two fire-dogs, admirable
specimens of the blacksmith's work.   Strange to say, on
the back of these, hidden from view, there were four
ornamental loops.

One November morning I lay reading in bed in my
London home, for the purpose of writing a review, the
latest of that fascinating series of books *A History
of Everyday Things in England*, by Mr. and Mrs. Quen-
nell.   The volume contained a reproduction of a Row-
landson drawing, showing a cottage interior of about
1800.   There was a group carousing by the window.
Near the large fireplace a woman sat watching a joint
being roasted on a spit.

Old Fireplace, Dining Room

The details of the rest of the picture told me all I wanted to know. High up near the ceiling there was a cage. It had a tread-wheel which held a dog. From the axle came two cords which passed through a slot at the right end of the mantelshelf and went down to a large wheel on the end of the spit-iron. In the rack above rested another long spit-iron. The slot in my mantelshelf was for the cords of a dog turnspit, the rack above had held the spits, which rested when in use on the loops behind the dog-irons.

I was so excited by this discovery that in half an hour I had the car out and was on my way to Pilgrim Cottage. On arriving there I had no further doubt of the solution, for in the slot I found two grooves chafed by the cords from the turnspit. The 'powder' cupboard was, of course, for the cooking salt.

Cooking and lighting both made demands on the blacksmith's craft. Pots, pans and fire-irons revealed his skill and artistry. Long before the age of brass candlesticks, he had made the rushlight-holders. Candles were not used for lighting until the early years of the Eighteenth Century. Up till about 1730 the only light known in cottages came from rushes, gathered by the village pond and dipped in grease. Shakespeare himself had written by rushlight, and this was the light he probably read by in the long winter evenings of his retirement at Stratford-on-Avon.

Grand old William Cobbett has a full description in his *Cottage Economy* of the rushlights made by his grandmother. 'She lived to be pretty nearly ninety, and never, I believe, burnt a candle in her house in her life.   I know that I never saw one there and she, in a great measure, brought me up.'

A good rush, two feet and a half in length, if dipped in mutton fat, burnt for an hour.   There were extravagant people, it seems, in the good old rush days.   Said Gilbert White in 1775, alluding to the fact that a poor family could enjoy five and a half hours of comfortable rushlight for a farthing—'Little farmers use rushes much in the short days, both morning and evening, in the dairy and kitchen, but the very poor, who are always the worst economists, and, therefore, must continue very poor, buy a half-penny candle every evening which, in their blowing, open rooms, does not burn much more than two hours.   Thus they have only two hours' light for their money instead of eleven.'   It would seem the road to bankruptcy was lit by candle-light.

The blacksmith made the rushlight-holder.   It was simple and ingenious.   A weighted base supported a long upright which terminated in two arms like a pair of scissors.   One of these arms was weighted and the rush was nipped between them.   It was a simple operation to push up the rush as it burned away.

Curious to learn what kind of light was obtained from a rush, I cut some rushes from a bank of the Thames, peeled them down to their pith, leaving one skin, and dipped them in mutton fat.   I stored them for a month before using.   I found that it was quite possible to read a newspaper by two rushlights.   A yard away they seemed only to light the darkness.   Anyone desiring a blaze of light and burning two dozen must have been kept busy moving the rushes up the holders, but doubtless anyone living in such a blaze of glory was deemed to be as mad as he was extravagant. A little experience of mediæval light begins to explain the emphasis laid upon the shining quality of angels. Glory, in eyes accustomed to a dismal scene, naturally took the form of light.

One experiment of rushlight was enough, but the ancient holder still has its use; it holds a candle, for the blacksmith, in the transitional age when the tallow candle began to come into fashion, turned the weighted arm into a socket. Users could therefore burn rushes or candles as they pleased, but if the latter they had to go to the smith for a pair of snuffers, which he now began to make with his usual skill.

Since we are around the fireplace let me introduce Miss Sophie and Miss Belinda. They would be out of place on the old kitchen mantelshelf, so they live in the study. They are two delightful young ladies in Anchor china, dressed in the fashionable silk sack dresses of the Eighteenth Century, with delicate feet peeping out from voluminous skirts. Miss Sophie generously exposes her tender bosom, but since she is dressed to represent Summer, her deep décolleté is as excusable as it is entrancing. Miss Belinda is a little more heavily clad, since she represents Winter.

They were a housewarming gift from Muriel Hine, who sent a note saying that if I was in doubt as to which was Winter and which was Summer, I had only to look underneath. Obeying this mysterious instruction I looked and discovered that while Miss Belinda, as Winter, was well clad, Miss Sophie, as Summer, wore no 'undies' at all!

I have begun to make a collection of face-brasses, to hang along the front of the mantelpiece. These brasses were buckled into the bridle front and gleamed on the horse's forehead. They perpetuate an ancient tradition when every horse carried an amulet on its forehead. The antiquity of this custom can be traced on the harness of the horses shown in the Assyrian stelæ at the British Museum.

Some of these brass ornaments were fastened on a wide leather strap hung from the collar, martingale, backband or withers. They can still be seen on brewers' and railway companies' drayhorses, but, with the horses, they are rapidly disappearing. There is one drawback to the collection of these brasses, as of other brasses—their cleaning will provoke a protest from the kitchen. There was a time when I sighed for a brass coal-scuttle. Someone told me that the Caledonian Market would provide a choice. It did, and I returned in triumph with a magnificent specimen. It happened to be at a time when the unlamented Mrs. T. carried the woes of the earth on her shoulders, and resented my coming to the cottage even for weekends.

"What an ugly thing!" she said, when I proudly produced it. "They've quite gone out—and who's going to clean it?"

This question demanded an obvious answer, and I realised it was time, now the scuttle had come in, for Mrs. T. to go out. I felt grateful to the scuttle for precipitating a crisis. My brasses shine now as brightly as the face of their cleaner.

WINTER NIGHT

When Winter comes and the lamp is lit,
When my poplars shiver, all warm I sit;
    The log fire leaps,
    The kettle sings,
    The puppy dog sleeps,
    And I dream of things.

Five thousand moons this old house knows,
Through Summers' droughts and Winters' snows—
    Why fret with thought
    Of pounds and pence?
    Soon I'll be nought
    And hurried hence.

The fire settles, and through a pane
I see a moon made new again;
    I hear a creak
    Upon the stair,
    Useless to seek
    If someone's there!

But if, perchance, poor lonely ghost,
This was your house where I'm now host,
    Come in and doze
    Beside the fire,
    And warm your toes
    To your heart's desire.

CHAPTER XVI

I

It is time for us to go into the garden again. Since it is now October its beauty is one of tints rather than flowers. The untidy season has begun; every morning the lawn is littered, and I notice the worms have begun tugging the leaves into the ground, which means that if I do not sweep up almost every day I shall have to go down on my knees and pick out the leaves the besom will not move.

It is berry time and dahlia time, but my garden is most noticeable for its banks of Michaelmas daisies and chrysanthemums. These awaken a boy's memory of colliers, and by implication, D. H. Lawrence! For I recall how, in the very village in Nottinghamshire, almost a town of depressing gloom and dirt, where the author of *Sons and Lovers* grew up, I used to see on Sunday mornings the colliers walking home from their allotment gardens carrying great bouquets of chrysanthemums. A shivering whippet generally clung to their heels, and if you entered the bar of any 'pub' open at noon, the table would look like a flower-show with the bouquets deposited while the owners were 'having one.' The collier has a great love of flowers, and the neat allotment gardens provided refreshing patches of colour in a countryside disfigured with pit heads, railway sidings and mountainous slag heaps.

There is one dahlia show that few private gardeners can compete with, the annual display in St. James's Park. There is nothing more glorious than those banked masses of blooms of endless variety that turn their blaze of colour towards Queen Anne's Gate. As this show takes place when the London park is beginning to be a little 'weepy' in the shortened days, the cheerfulness is all the greater.

The gardening in the London Parks is a form of cheating, let us admit. The Parks are not gardens, but places for bedding-out flowers in bloom. The pageant is a swift one and ceaselessly changing. The flowers at the first sign of withering are whisked away, and new plants occupy their places. The strange thing is that one so seldom catches the gardeners at it. Do they work at night, are they up at dawn? Once I did see them, removing rhododendron trees. It was late evening, and in the dusk I was walking through St. James's Park with a waggish friend. I can still see the amazement on the faces of the gardeners as he paused by the railings, and, admonishing them with an umbrella, cried—"Naughty! Naughty! Stealing the public's plants!"

And here let me make a protest against the too-country-minded, a class generally drawn from town week-enders, whose enthusiasm often stops short with trundling a wheelbarrow or digging a trench, or saying—"Ah, Thomson, the what-d'you-call-'ems are coming on very nicely. We'll plant more next year."

I am a London lover. I have lived in many cities, in various lands, and it is not narrow patriotism that makes me declare London to be without a peer for dignity, beauty, convenience and variety. Lovely as is the Bois de Boulogne, it lacks the spacious charm of grass and plane trees, and the quick contrast of street and park. The Bois is always a little Watteauish, a little 'coiffured.'

I do not love my country garden any the less because I am often thrilled by the trick gardening of the London Parks. It is so well done, it never descends to the meretricious, as in that Jezebel of towns, Monte Carlo, where the palm trees bloom with festoons of lanterns, and every bush is afire, not with God, but with electric bulbs.

The Londoner is rightly proud of his Parks, and they are an excellent example of the Englishman's genius for compromise. The Royal Parks were the property of the Crown. Queen Caroline, observing the custom of foreign monarchs, who shut or opened their Parks and gardens as their moods suited, had a thought of closing Kensington Gardens, and enquired of Walpole the probable cost. "Only a crown, Madam," he replied, and wisely the Queen thought it better to retain the throne and let the gardens go. We have made a mess of many things, and lost superb chances, as a walk along the Thames Embankment will show, but London is unrivalled in the possession of her Parks, where the Scottish shepherd can be seen, from the top of a Piccadilly bus, herding sheep.

And what traditions and foreign influences can be traced in our Parks! They hold most known examples of formal and natural gardening, from the Dutch garden at Kensington, to the Athenian 'academy' at Cumberland Gate, where oratory and debate flourish.

One can walk like a courtier of Versailles by the ornamental gardens of Long Water, swim on the Lido of the
Serpentine, or please an equestrian mood in Rotten Row.
There are green swards, shaded by noble trees, that,
dotted with gallants and their ladies, would have pleased
Watteau, and I have found vistas that would have
given delight to Constable or Corot. I have even penetrated into the nursery garden, well hidden, where the
floral surprises of the Parks are mostly nourished.

Even the Persian tradition is present, that mingling
of flowers and beasts in Paradise, which is the theme of
their carpets. The Persians were poets in their gardens
and gardening, and while we have no jewelled birds, we
have other constituents of that marvellous garden carpet,
measuring nearly a quarter of an acre, found by the
sons of the Prophet when they took Ctesiphon in A. D.
637, for the lions, boars, stags, antelopes, monkeys,
snakes and jackals of the Persian carpet are found in
Regent's Park. It was E. V. Lucas who noticed the
comprehensive nature of London Parks and gardens.
'Battersea Park is for games; St. James's Park for water-
fowl; the Green Park for repose; Hyde Park for fashion
and horsemanship; Kensington Gardens for children
and toy-boats; and Regent's Park for botany and wild
beasts.'

No, I will not hear a sneer against the gardens and
Parks of London. No honest countryman will exhibit
such bad taste. The scorn is always born of a sudden
passion for the country in the fickle heart of a town-
dweller. The countryman is filled with admiration
of these heroic window boxes, these gay parterres,
cat-haunted, soot-saturated, with which the Londoner

beautifies his terrain.   One of the most flourishing vines I ever saw, with healthy bunches of grapes, was in a Bermondsey slum.   Through long years it had been skilfully trained over an outhouse.

A housing expert, interested in slum clearance, astonished me by saying that opposition was always strongest where the tenant had to forsake some half-alive tree, a wall of Virginia creeper, or a diminutive 'garden-plot,' where a few blades of grass or an odd bulb struggled to the light.   No social worker can compete with Woolworth's in the task of brightening the slums.   I have seen Limehouse ablaze with 'unimaginable' flowers and heard canaries trilling amid brave bowers of blossom in tenements where four persons lived in a room.

II

October is renowned for the richness of its autumn tints, but with the shifting of the seasons is not November now the month when Death passes in sublime pageantry through the woods?   From my garden I looked upwards to an amphitheatre of beechwoods. They were glorious in October, but November gave them the richest hues.   With what golden fire they flamed above me, facing the setting sun!   The lane leading to the parkland where I often walk, lit by the wintry sunlight, had a glory it had never known in April or June.   Here was a marvellous range of greens and russets shining against the cold blue sky.   The oak and the ash varied the tones of gold, and here and there a plantation of larch and fir stood densely at the plateau's edge, in a sharp contrast of pale yellow and dark green. The field before it, radiant as Youth at the feet of Age, shone with the vivid green of winter wheat.

This is the time when the gardener's notes in the newspapers and magazines are positively threatening. You must dig and trench, you must manure and mulch, you are perhaps already too late to plan your garden nearer to your heart's desire. In despair you discover that the bed, so jumbled in June, so empty of flowers in August, which you had intended thinning and varying, is now a barren mystery. Is this a delphinium, phlox, thistle or golden-rod which you are digging up? It is one thing to know the appearance of flowers, it is quite another to know their roots. Your bright surface intelligence is of no use in this underground world. In despair you dig and throw out, and perhaps next summer, unless you are very clever and careful, you will discover that the nicely graduated bed slopes away from you to the hedge, and that, sitting on the lawn, you are in the 'gods,' and cannot see the stage set with pansies, violas and thrift because of a row of tall fat-headed thistles, or flaunting red-hatted poppies that block your view. Unless you are a clever 'rooter' there is only one way to avoid this trouble. You must be a remorseless cutter-out in the high season of blooms. Then you know what you are doing. A ruthless June may save you a perplexed November.

III

On the last day of November I walked round my garden. My back ached, my hands were blistered. The last of the beds had been dug over. Barrow-loads of cow dung had been wheeled from the farm, and horse manure from the stable at the large house opposite. I learned, incidentally, to be a little more tolerant of a young man I had regarded with dislike. This house, so long unlet because it is of the six-servant standard, possesses a groom's cottage and a stable. Recently a hunter had been kept in the stable, looked after by the groom in the adjacent cottage. Now, although I come of Leicestershire stock, I have no enthusiasm for the Yoick! Halloo! crowd that goes ruinously over the fallow fields, and pursues to a gory end the wretched fox. There is enough natural cruelty in the world without manufacturing it; but perhaps I am funny that way.

I had observed with coolness the tall young man whose motor horse-van delivered his hunter at the stable opposite, who sometimes arrived in one of those excessively long-bonneted cars that suggest an excessively long purse. He was elegant in leggings, breeches and yellow waistcoat. He had an officer-class voice in commanding his servants, and a young Guardsman's suavity in addressing the friends who sat in his saloon, coupé or sports car.

Chance once led us into conversation and I reluctantly found him affable. But my disapproval remained. I disliked his pastime, at once cruel and callously expensive. This transporting of horses by motor-van, this monogramed blanketing and puppy-walking, when millions were pinched, ill-clad, ill-housed, troubled my social conscience, not tranquillised by the specious argument that the excess of one is good for the poverty of thousands.

One day a distressful noise invaded my garden. There could be no doubt what it was. Few animals have been so ill-treated by man and Nature as the donkey. Its voice is a hideous protest to Fate. It was this protest at intervals that sent me indignantly up to my sun platform to observe the orchard opposite. Yes, there in the orchard of the empty house stood a donkey! Why he should fill the air with hee-hawing, I could not say. Only a donkey would protest against such a lush paradise of grass and fruit.

When I went to enquire about manure at the groom's cottage a pungent, acrid odour from a horsebox caused me to look in. The upper half of the door was wired, and I saw to my great surprise a vixen and four cubs. They crouched, motionless, with staring eyes, sharp ears and noses, watching me with the suspicious hostility of an animal that knows it is the hunted enemy of man. And when one cub retreated and observed me from round the back of a box, I saw then how right was the term 'crafty' when applied to the fox. Nevertheless, I had pity in my heart as I walked on to the groom's cottage. I almost reproached myself for buying the manure of this establishment.

The bargain concluded, a painful hee-haw across the orchard made me comment on the donkey.

"Ay, sir, he's come from London," said the groom. "He belonged to a fish hawker down in Poplar, and he was sick and lame. The master was so sorry for him, he bought him and sent him here, and he ain't half in clover! That's just like the master. He's the softest-hearted lad that ever walked, sir!"

I said not a word, paid for the manure, and went away. "Hee-haw, hee-haw!" cried the donkey. Yes, the laugh was certainly against me. How difficult it is to judge one's fellow men!

IV

One of the autumn's problems is hedge-mending. There are two painful gaps in my hedge, and whenever I see them they evoke memories somewhat bitter. Not far distant lives a worthy dairy farmer. He has the reputation of being an independent fellow. Conflicts with him have left strained relations in the village, and they are the more strained because he has always contrived to have the better of the dispute. A neighbour's dog chases his chickens in the adjacent field, and the pet is threatened with a gun. The cows that after calving are turned out, and fill the air with a mournful lament through the night and prevent sleep, must needs eat some yew clippings left by a careless gardener. This time the aggrieved neighbour has to pay, highly indignant because he is undoubtedly in the wrong. It seems folly that a man should attempt to farm in a place where inevitably he must fight encroaching civilisation. He could reply that he was there first.

Anyhow, I have the deepest respect for him. His kind are the backbone of England. He is thrifty and hard-working. His wife and family all labour with him. Every morning his son drives the milk-float along the lane at the bottom of my hedge. I can just see his curled head, open throat and strong shoulders over the hedge. He passes, like a young Apollo, driving the chariot of the Dawn.

But there are incidents not so poetic. One lovely June afternoon I was reading in the garden. A noise in the lane told me that the cows were being taken out to pasture. The state of that lane in winter after cows had traversed it twice daily had caused me to enquire into closure rights. I found I possessed these, but as this entailed a detour for the farmer, and I wish to live amicably with my neighbours, I had done nothing in the matter, though often irritated by the muddy state of the lane.

This afternoon something made me look up from a book to find myself confronted by a bewildered cow. There it stood in the middle of my garden bed, a frightful gap in the broken hedge behind. Paralysed with horror, I stared back at the wretched cow. But worse was to follow. Two more cows came through the gap, and after them an excited cowherd. The alarm given, the farmer and his son came in through my gate. I think we must all have lost our heads, for we tried to chase the cows out through the gap. They refused to go; instead, they began plunging up and down my garden beds. Two of them, harried by a dog, made a complete circuit of the house, their hooves pitting the lawn wherever they went.

The young cowherd, in his excitement, seized a cow by the horns and began wrestling with it. This herculean attempt ended in complete disaster, for the frightened cow plunged worse than ever. In the space of five minutes my garden and lawn were wrecked. It was no use attempting to herd the cows out of the garden, there was little to save. Broken delphiniums, phlox, rosebushes, lupins, kicked up thrift, a pitted lawn—everywhere the ruin had spread. I implored them to stop the chase, and opened wide the garden gate. So far the cows had not crashed through my windows. Perhaps left alone they would find their way out by the gate. We waited and eventually they did. The farmer and his assistants followed. The scene around me was pitiful. A Spartan would have burst into tears.

A few minutes elapsed and the farmer reappeared.

"I'm very sorry about this," he said contritely. "I'll pay for the damage."

"It's obvious your cows were not properly herded," I said.

"One's rather frisky."

"I am afraid I shall have to raise the question of your using this lane. I've put up with the nuisance, as I've no wish to make your job difficult, but if——"

The farmer's jaw set, and the Mr. Towser who had warred with others emerged at once.

"I know the law—that's a public lane, and I shall use it as I want. You can't frighten me with your lawyers; no, you can't! I know as much law as they do and——"

"In that case, Mr. Towser, don't let's discuss it further. We'll put the matter to a test."

"We will!" he shouted.

He stumped off, but at the gate halted and called:

"I'll send one of the boys to straighten up."

"Straighten up?" I said, icily.   "You've done enough damage here already.   The damage will be repaired as much as possible, and you'll have the bill."

"All right—but I know the law, I do!" repeated Farmer Towser, and went out.

"Your tea is ready, sir," said Mrs. Bean, my house-keeper, almost in tears.

I went indoors, hot, indignant and revengeful.

Farmer Towser's knowledge of law was, I suspected, amateurish.   Moreover, I had already procured a firm opinion based on my land titles, and all this apart, if we committed the folly of feeing lawyers, I was better equipped for ruinous battle.

But in my heart I had no desire for battle, or to provoke a hard-working man into an expensive action. Although neither the conduct of his cows nor of himself had been pleasant, I had felt sorry for the farmer.   He was in the wrong and knew it.   He was an honest man, independent and indefatigable.   I have the deepest respect for any man wringing a livelihood from the soil. If Farmer Towser had only known, despite his attitude, he was one of my heroes.

So I did nothing.   I did not even send him a bill for damages.   That he was troubled with his conscience I knew by the fact that before I rose next morning he had boarded up the gap in my fence.   The garden and hedge, of course, did not wholly recover that summer.

Two months later, after absence in Paris, Louis and myself returned to London.   Impatient to see Pilgrim Cottage again, we motored down at night.   The next morning, immediately on rising, we went out into our loved garden. What we found there rooted us in speechless horror. The scene of devastation of two months ago was repeated! There was a terrible gap in the hedge, the flower-beds were trampled down, and in these and in the lawn all round the house there were hoof-marks six inches deep. On enquiry I found that the cows had broken in the previous evening. My housekeeper had not dared to dash our pleasure and spoil our sleep by giving us the news.

Well, this was a grim business. My tolerance had been tried beyond further endurance. Stern action would have to be taken against Farmer Towser. I was considering in what manner to proceed when the farmer was announced.

I went out to interview him in an icy mood. But when I saw him he was such a picture of contrition that all my wrath evaporated. He said he had no excuses to make, he could only offer a full apology, and pay for the damage done. It seemed that a frisky calf had plunged through the weak part of the hedge when the herd had been stemmed by a passing lorry in the main road. The mother had immediately followed the calf. In future he would have the cattle haltered and led. He only desired to live in peace with his neighbours and act fairly.

All this said, he again suggested that I should have the damage repaired and the bill sent to him. It had been on my tongue to tell him that I should close the road to cattle, action or no action, but I felt I could not carry on a war with a man so sorry for himself.

I agreed to send him the bill. But I did not, and when, meeting me a month later, he asked about it, I charged him a day's wages of the gardener as a token payment. Meanwhile, he had erected a fence so substantial that a toreador could have sought refuge behind it.

Now, on this autumn afternoon, as I looked at the gaps in the hedge, with thoughts of renovation during the winter, those cow invasions came back to mind. I decided to buy two large privets, as the variation of colour, light green, olive, bronze and gold, is very pleasing to the eye. In places I have allowed the hawthorn to sprout into a small tree, which gives me blossom in the spring, and red berries in the autumn.

This year, after a wonderful summer, there were magnificent crops of berries. Up the lane, where I had just been for a walk, the hedge tops had a scarlet haze where the berry clusters shone through the dull air. And never before had I seen such a profusion of that last embellishment of the hedgerows, old man's beard or traveller's joy. The former name is much more realistic and seasonable. The traveller's joy is somewhat dimmed these days, when the leafless hedges show their iron skeletons, and old man's beard really does suggest the advent of Father Christmas, with traditional whiskers.

There is one last drama in my garden for which I always wait, hoping it will be enacted while I am present, and not during absence in London. It really rings down the curtain on the autumn. In the corner of the garden stands a young chestnut tree. It gives a splendid shade in the glare of summer. Through the winter its sticky mahogany buds hold promise of the future spring. In the late autumn its broad leaves change to golden yellow, and when all the colours have faded in the garden it stands there, a maiden in a bright party frock among all the greybeards.

Each November evening, on drawing the blinds after lamplight has come, I look out on the chestnut, for it has a habit of holding the last glow of sunset in the unseen sky. Also, I never know but that I may be seeing its glory for the last time. One morning I rise and behold—the chestnut stands naked to the sky, its autumn frock all tumbled about its feet. A night-frost has completely stripped the poor thing, and the apple trees, the poplars and laburnums, still in a process of leaf-losing, look pityingly at their naked sister, who only yesterday evening was so proud of herself. There is nothing now but to fetch a sack, stuff the leaves in it, and carry them to the garden bonfire. Experience has taught me the folly of filling the wheelbarrow. A sudden wind round the garden, and one's labour has been all in vain.

TO A CHESTNUT FOUND
STRIPPED

Poor lady, I could weep for your distress,
   How rude of Winter to have stripped you so,
Tumbling about your feet your lovely dress,
   Leaving you naked to the winds that blow.

Poor lady, who was once all dressed in gold,
   Take heart, have you not heard the whispering?
Before the New Year's patterns all were sold
   Time placed an order with the looms of Spring.

Dear lady, you will burst with pride in May
   When you put on the new dress made for you,
A crinoline, with candle-flowers gay,
   A lovely green to match the Spring sky's blue.

CHAPTER XVII

DA CAPO

I

THE close of the year brings a final survey before the frost and the hardened ground prevent further labour. And I must come to a final decision this sad November month. There is an old plum tree long past service. Two of its branches are withered, and I have never seen fruit on it. But it is fantastic in shape, the birds seem to like it, and autumn after autumn I have reprieved it. I cling to an old tree like an old tooth, and am reluctant to tear it out by the roots, leaving a horrid gap. But it really must go, and in anticipation I have been to the nurseryman and bought a healthy cherry tree, a Morello, that will be as much appreciated by the birds as by myself.

By the oddest circumstances I was encouraged to let my fancy run riot at the nurseryman's. Just as the car was ticking over at the door ready for departure, a letter arrived from the bank. Should I open it and spoil my afternoon? What dividend had failed me this time, what profit-bearing tree planted in Australia, New Zealand, Canada or elsewhere had failed to produce its seasonal fruit? So many trees had been barren this year, so many had suffered from the American blight.

But courage! I tore open the envelope and learned

the most surprising of all news. The bank informed me that there had been deposited to my account a rebate of income-tax. It transpired that some years ago, a kind Australian public having assimilated large numbers of a novel I had almost forgotten, tax had been levied in excess of the subsequent rate. Now, after three years, some it it had returned.

Manna from heaven was not more miraculous. It was with difficulty that the nurseryman hid his surprise at the levity with which I ordered everything he assured me would blossom or bear fruit. Australia, God bless her, should make a blaze in my garden. When we came to the topiary garden, with a green menagerie of yews and box trees, I asked him if he had a kangaroo, but the nearest I could get to a national symbol was a peacock, which I might call a lyre-bird, and thus honour the Southern Continent.

For the gap in the hedge I bought a cypressus, a hornbeam and a quickthorn. Tea with two maiden ladies at Newbury last spring had given me an unforgettable memory of a forsythia falling like golden rain over their garden wall, so I bought a *Forsythia suspensa*. On my list there was a jolly purple buddleia bush. For some reason friends always laugh when I ask them if they've seen a buddleia bush. They think it must be a kind of joke. Why is it not better known? I bought another because of the butterflies and bees that haunt the corner of the garden where it stands. All through the summer there literally was not alighting room on the long pyramidal spike of lavender-coloured flowers. Over the whole of its ten feet there was a constant hum of bee and butterfly traffic. It is not a plant for a quiet corner of the garden, but it is a constant joy to the eye, the nose and the insects.

As the nurseryman led me through his beds and recited the names of all the things that would make next year lovely, I began wondering who gave such names to plants and shrubs, and how one obtained a dedication, say, of a rose or a lupin. As an author I have at times been the dedicator and the dedicatee, but surely it must be a much more thrilling experience to go through Time allied with a rosebush or a tulip? Immortal Dorothy Perkins, Maréchal Niel and Wm. Allen Richardson, for ever blooming and fading, loved in a thousand vicarage gardens!

Well, quite unofficially I have named a plant. There is a pale mauve delphinium called 'Sir Arthur Hazlerigg,' known to gardeners. There is also a cornflower-blue delphinium called 'Sir Richard Roberts,' unknown by this name to gardeners, for I christened it.

The reason for it calls up an episode of the Civil War, when families and old friendships were split in twain. Sir Arthur and Sir Richard were neighbours in Leicestershire. They had been High Sheriffs, their families had intermarried. Sir Arthur espoused the Parliamentarian cause; Sir Richard, the Royalist. In the troubled year of 1642 Sir Arthur rode to Newcastle to hold it for Cromwell, but before he went he visited his old friend for the last time.

Sir Richard, aged seventy-nine, rode to the raising of the Royal standard, forty miles away at Nottingham, in the presence of King Charles. Was it prophetic of the ill-fated cause that it was blown down in the night following that windy autumn day? Old Sir Richard died in the midst of the strife. Sir Arthur lived to see the Restoration, was flung into the Tower, and died there. Now they rest, not far apart, in the heart of their domains, Sir Richard at Church Langton, Sir Arthur at Noseley.

I do not know who named a delphinium 'Sir Arthur Hazlerigg.' There is still a Sir Arthur at Noseley. But I thought it only fitting that the Sir Arthur in my garden should have the company of Sir Richard. In June these two proud delphiniums make a glorious show, and one's admiration is divided between the sturdy Parliamentarian and the old Royalist, sharing the peace of the garden.

II

My gardener looked alarmed when the parcels arrived from the nursery. "I hope, sir, you've done?" he asked. I assured him I had, perhaps falsely. For the garden lover can never be done. Nature pours her cornucopia over him and he clutches at this lovely thing, at that lovely thing. Next year his garden will be different, even more beautiful. He can never rest on his laurels. Every autumn he must dig and plan, every spring he must plant and prick out. In December he may pause a little, but only to gird himself for Nature's unfailing return.

Years ago, when my small fingers were painfully driven over the sharps and flats of the family piano, I would come to the end of troublesome Czerny, with his Hundred and One Exercises, or of Clementi with his tricky sonatas. And then, at the very end, I would find two Italian words, *Da Capo*. "That," said my music mistress, "means back to the beginning again."

Back to the beginning again. Yes, but this time with what anticipation, what happiness! It is the close of a November afternoon. The high beechwoods are aglow in the misty air. Around me there are spirals of smoke rising like votive offerings from my neighbours' garden fires.

I look at the old house. It has stood thus through the November days of these past four hundred years. It may stand for yet another four hundred. It has been 'home' for generations who have looked on these same hills, laboured in this garden, swept up and burnt the autumnal leaves. In a few minutes I shall enter and close my door. There will be tea and toast, and I shall delay lighting the lamp the better to enjoy the play of firelight on the old beams and walls, and see through the misting panes the crimson flush in a fading sky. Soon Mrs. Bean will enter with the tea tray, and will place the tea-pot in its chintz cosy on the table.

"Shall I light the lamp, sir?" she will ask.

"No, Mrs. Bean, not yet, thank you."

She will look at the fire, sweep up a little ash, and then glance out of the window. I know what is coming.

"The nights do draw in, sir!"

"They do, Mrs. Bean."

"And to think it will soon be Christmas again!"

Thereupon she goes. And though she has reminded me of mortality, that Time flies, I am not unhappy; for there rings in my mind the question, and the anticipation, of the poet—

If Winter comes, can Spring be far behind?

(1)